Children & Nature
Making Connections

Edited by

George K. Russell

The Myrin Institute
187 Main Street
Great Barrington, MA 01230
(413) 528-8135
www.myrin.org

Cover and book design by Ann Erwin
Cover image by Cultura RM/Julia Kuskin

ISBN #978-0-980083-11-8

Printed by McNaughton & Gunn, Inc.
Saline, MI USA

CONTENTS

Making Connections: The need and the challenge 7
George K. Russell

Leave No Child Inside: The growing movement to reconnect
children and nature 16
Richard Louv

The Human Touch 28
Lowell Monke

Look, Don't Touch: The problem with environmental education 38
David Sobel

An Indian Father's Plea 54
Medicine Grizzlybear Lake

Tokens of Mystery. 60
Scott Russell Sanders

Lessons of a Starry Night 73
Kelly McMasters

Cradle 81
Pattiann Rogers

Toddlers to Tweens: Relearning how to play. 92
Stephanie Hanes

The Privilege of Gardening with Children 102
Carolyn Jabs

Words Full of Wonder 112
James E. Higgins

A Wilderness of Thought: Childhood and the poetic imagination 125
Richard Lewis

Contributors 134

Suggestions 138

Credits 140

About the Myrin Institute 142

George K. Russell

MAKING CONNECTIONS
The need and the challenge

AS A LONGTIME INSTRUCTOR of university-level biology students, I regularly meet young people whose chief interest is the study of cellular and molecular processes, but have little acquaintance with living nature and little or no inclination to study the life sciences in a more integrated or holistic manner. There are, to be sure, numerous exceptions and our course offerings in ecology, vertebrate zoology, and animal behavior draw students with interests in field-based studies and the biology of whole organisms. I am especially heartened to find an occasional student who has spent countless hours of childhood outside in nature or one who has tended a vegetable garden and hatched butterflies. But my long experience with students concentrating in biology and a wide variety of non-majors is that many if not most have had little meaningful experience of the natural world. I am troubled by what I see as a profound disconnect between the world of nature and the interests and inclinations of so many young people, and I can foresee consequences if this matter is not taken seriously and addressed in all earnestness.

At the heart of the issue is the notion that direct personal encounter with nature, and the attendant feelings of wonder and delight, form the basis of a genuine ethos for protection of the natural environment. We will honor and preserve what we have come to love and admire, and such feelings find their source in personal experience. But what of those for whom there is little or no connection with nature? Can we expect them to participate with enthusiasm in the search for solutions to the vast array of environmental problems confronting us? And are we losing sight of the idea that each individual has the possibility of finding in the myriad wonders of nature an opportunity for self-renewal and inspiration?

My own approach is to introduce, where possible, an admixture of natural history into my several courses, including definite assignments in the close observation of living nature in whatever ways I can arrange. We may not be able to visit the rainforests of Amazonia or Yosemite National Park, but we can make use of local habitats, the university campus itself, and what the ecologist David Ehrenfeld has called "the rainforests of home." Whatever successes I have had convince me that students will take a deeper interest in the study of the living world, both inside and beyond the classroom, if they are guided to an authentic encounter with living plants and animals, natural settings, and the enchantments of life itself.

But the concern for my own students has far broader implications. My personal observations do not stand in isolation. The present collection has been assembled out of a deep concern that many young people in America have so little contact with the world of nature. A generation that spends, on average, 7 hours 38 minutes each day on some sort of screen (hand-held, video, TV, etc.)[1] will have no time for quiet immersion in a natural setting, no time to play in nature, no time to experience the tides or the vicissitudes of the weather or the comings and goings of wild animals or the resurgence of life in the spring. Recent surveys show that many young people in this country can identify up to a hundred corporate logos but cannot name or describe even five species of songbirds, wild animals or common flowers.

I hope the essays in this book will awaken in readers the wish to assist young people by showing them what lies outside their front door or in a local park or woodland, and that true nature experience will come to replace what is surely a powerful form of addiction, a dependency on text messages, e-mails and videos and a torrent of unreal, virtual images. A challenge stands squarely before us: How can we begin to address the malaise of indifference to nature so widespread among our young people? The implications for the future of not doing so, to my mind, are quite beyond imagining.

The task before us is immense. One of my principal efforts has been to identify significant readings that highlight various elements of the issue and bring these to the attention of the students in my classes, concerned teachers, environment educators, parents and all those who see the need for a vast change in the way we raise and educate our children. The articles offered here have been tried and tested with university students, especially those who are about to enter the field of teaching, and I have found many individuals who, in full sympathy, recognize both the need and the challenge.

The keystone of the effort is Richard Louv's book, *Last Child in the Woods: Saving Our Children from Nature-Deficit Disorder*. Louv asserts that profound nature experience is a "spiritual necessity" for the growing child, but that the youngster who plays outdoors, like the Florida panther and the whooping crane, has become a kind of endangered species, in his words the "last child in the woods." A fourth-grader in San Diego put the matter very succinctly: "I like to play indoors better 'cause that's where all the electrical outlets are." Richard Louv quotes the naturalist, Robert Michael Pyle, who asks poignantly: "What is the extinction of a condor to a child who has never seen a wren?" and Louv looks to the future with great concern, asking, "Where then will the stewards of nature come from?" Included in the present collection are Louv's thoughtful reflections following the publication of his book and the long series of talks he has given to parent groups, teachers, outdoor educators, young people and concerned citizens. The movement to which he has contributed so substantially is often referred to, appropriately, as "No Child Left Inside."

Lowell Monke, another of the contributors to this collection, is a former Computer Sciences teacher in the public school system of Iowa and is now a faculty member in the Department of Education at Wittenberg University. His long experience as a teacher of the Computer Sciences has shown him both the value and the challenges of an increasingly computer-bound age. Monke has been a singular voice in showing that for every positive argument put forward in favor of computers in schools, there is a hidden, unrecognized loss. He argues that the digital screen cannot begin to simulate the direct experience of nature that Richard Louv reminds us is so very essential for the proper growth and development of a child. "Children come to know a tree," Monke writes, "by peeling its bark, climbing it branches, sitting under its shade, jumping into its piled-up leaves. Just as important, these firsthand experiences are enveloped by feelings and associations—muscles being used, sun warming the skin, blossoms scenting the air. The computer cannot even approximate any of this."

Personal experience of nature lies at the very heart of the issue. Individuals who are fortunate enough as children to have had profound connections with all that nature offers—plants, animals, wild places, natural rhythms, the sky and weather, and much else—will have a firm foundation that can extend throughout their lives. Scott Russell Sanders's moving account of his relation with his son speaks directly to this theme. In "Tokens of Mystery" Sanders writes that "If a child is to have an expansive and respectful vision of nature, there is no substitute for direct encounters with wildness. This means passing unprogrammed days and weeks in the mountains, the woods, the fields, beside rivers and oceans, territories where plants and beasts are the natives and we are the visitors."

David Sobel, author of "Look, Don't Touch: The problem with environmental education," has made numerous and substantial contributions to the field; his study, *Beyond Ecophobia: Reclaiming the Heart of Nature Education,* is widely cited and admired. Other books and articles of his carry themes relating to "place-based education" and are well known. In "Look, Don't Touch" he reminds us that childhood experience in nature is all-important in establishing lasting bonds between individuals and the natural world. He writes that John Muir, E.O. Wilson, Aldo Leopold and Rachel Carson all had "down-and-dirty experiences in childhood" that formed lifelong bonds with the earth and its creatures. Sobel tells us that "nature programs should invite children to make mud pies, climb trees, catch frogs, paint their faces with charcoal, get their hands dirty and their feet wet." Too much emphasis on concepts and the mechanical principles of nature, especially in the early years, does little to establish the sort of deep communion with nature to which he alludes. "Between the ages of six and twelve, learning about nature is less important that simply getting children out into nature."

"An Indian Father's Plea" by Medicine Grizzlybear Lake, a letter to his son's teacher, speaks to the very heart of education and nature experience. A Native American father is asking the teacher (and the reader) to consider what it means to know something and whether the boy's direct learning through experience in nature bears any relation to indoor classroom knowledge that forms so much of our educational system.

Rachel Carson is best known for her seminal work, *Silent Spring,* a book that helped to launch the environmental movement in the early 1970s, but she is also the author of "The Sense of Wonder," a lyrical essay she wrote a few years before her death in 1964. This article is currently under copyright protection and has not been reprinted here, but I urge readers to locate the work and judge its value for themselves.[2] "The Sense of Wonder" has been widely acclaimed as one of the great American nature essays and it deserves serious attention from everyone concerned for the future of the natural environment and the future of our children.

Carson spent her summer vacations at a cabin retreat along the coast of southeastern Maine where she found solace, repose and the inner strength to confront powerful voices not wanting to hear her messages about toxic chemicals and poisoning of the natural environment. In "The Sense of Wonder" she helps the reader recapture something of lost childhood and to reflect on the sense of wonder that each child brings into life as a kind of birthright. I trust that each reader of this essay will come to value even more the power of nature to awaken our hearts to the beauties and wonders of nature. Rachel Carson has alerted us to what we are doing to the natural environment; she has also shown us how in nature we can find sustenance for the human spirit.

A child's world is fresh and new and beautiful, full of wonder and excitement. It is our misfortune that for most of us that clear-eyed vision, that true instinct for what is beautiful and awe-inspiring, is dimmed and even lost before we reach adulthood. If I had influence with the good fairy who is supposed to preside over the christening of all children, I should ask that her gift to each child in the world be a sense of wonder so indestructible that it would last throughout life, as an unfailing antidote against the boredom and disenchantments of later years, the sterile preoccupation with things artificial, the alienation from the sources of our strength.

In the present collection Kelly McMasters writes about her dreadful experience in a car accident and her efforts to find healing, both physical and spiritual, following the event. Significantly, she uses the lessons of Rachel Carson's essay and their relation to the accident to enrich and better understand herself and especially to bring about a deeper connection with her young son. "Lessons of a Starry Night" carries the subtitle: "A Rachel Carson essay teaches a new mother how to imbue her growing child with an awe of nature."

Surely we must give far more attention to the role of parenting and the need for caring adults to foster compassion and love in children, especially during the formative years of early childhood. Pattiann Rogers writes in "Cradle" that "I cannot think of anything more important for the future of the earth than that we have loving, diligent mothers and fathers caring for our children. ...If children learn to act with compassion by being treated compassionately themselves, if they learn love by being loved, to respect others by having received respect, to cooperate by being involved in cooperation, to keep their word by experiencing honesty, to protect others by having been protected themselves, how can we possibly overestimate the importance of children being nurtured by dependable parents who are capable of demonstrating such qualities? It is these qualities that will form the basis for all future decisions our children must make regarding their interactions with other people and with the natural world."

One of the most troubling aspects of our theme is that children seem to have forgotten how to play. Stephanie Hanes writes in "Toddlers to Tweens" that for many if not most American children "free play" no longer exists. Youngsters are programmed and scheduled, tested and retested, given little or no recess time at school, and pressured to get ready for higher levels of education. They have little or no experience of the joys of wandering, the vagaries of fantasizing or the simple pleasures of made-up games, unscheduled days and the carefree delights of summer. Hanes writes that "children's play is threatened, and kids—from toddlers to tweens—should be relearning to play. Roughhousing and fantasy feed development." The matter of children's play is a serious concern for parents, teachers and child psychologists throughout this country. Many current books, popular magazines, and academic studies attest to this concern, and readers will likely be able to suggest titles of their own. I offer Gary Paul Nabhan and Stephen Trimble's *The Geography of Childhood: Why Children Need Wild Places*; Susan Linn's *The Case for Make Believe: Saving Play in a Commercialized World;* and the highly relevant publications of the Alliance for Childhood. The issues underlying these accounts and many others must find their way into the heart of current educational discourse and they deserve our fullest attention.

Along a similar vein, "The Privilege of Gardening with Children" by Carolyn Jabs speaks to the matter of children and the soil. Young people who cannot recognize various types of wild flowers, songbirds or species of ornamental trees and shrubs will not have planted seeds or harvested vegetables or picked apples. Jabs offers helpful, practical suggestions for how parents can guide youngsters in the planting and caring for a garden. Most importantly, she informs us that "children have a deep and abiding interest in growing, perhaps because they are doing it themselves. They remind us, if we let them, that the point of gardening is not a perfect platoon of well-disciplined plants. Rather, it is the privilege of witnessing a miracle as simple, profound, and unpredictable as growth itself."

Douglas Sloan, Professor Emeritus at Teachers College, Columbia, has written elsewhere that children "simply being in nature is not enough. If nature is to nourish children, and they in turn are to protect and nourish it as adults, imaginative capacities for feeling and perception must be brought to birth in childhood. Here the influence of word, story, poem and all the arts become of crucial importance. They work with nature in awakening imagination. The confidence and capacity to meet and care for life are called forth by an education suffused with the beauty and forces of life." In this spirit we have included two articles: James E. Higgins's "Words Full of Wonder," an essay on the value of children's literature and the influence of adults who share stories with a child, and Richard Lewis's piece on "A Wilderness of Thought: Childhood and the Poetic Imagination," a wonderful account of poetry and the children who write it.

I leave the final words for Rachel Carson who speaks directly to the major theme of this collection. When asked by parents how they can teach youngsters about the natural world when they themselves know so very little about it, her answer was the following:

> If a child is to keep alive his inborn sense of wonder without any such gift from the fairies, he needs the companionship of at least one adult who can share it, rediscovering with him the joy, excitement and mystery of the world we live in. Parents often have a sense of inadequacy when confronted on the one hand with the eager, sensitive mind of a child and on the other with a world of complex physical nature, inhabited by a life so various and unfamiliar that it seems hopeless to reduce it to order and knowledge. In a mood of self-defeat, they exclaim, "How can I possibly teach my child about nature—why, I don't even know one bird from another." I sincerely believe that for the child, and for the parent seeking to guide him, it is not half so important to know as to feel. If facts are the seeds that later produce knowledge and wisdom, then the emotions and years of early childhood are the time to prepare the soil. Once the emotions have been aroused—a sense of the beautiful; the excitement of the new and the unknown; a feeling of sympathy, pity, admiration or love—then we wish for knowledge about the object of our emotional response. Once found, it has lasting meaning. It is more important to pave the way for the child to want to know than to put him on a diet of facts he is not ready to assimilate.

Rachel Carson tells us that "those who dwell among the beauties and mysteries of the earth are never alone or weary of life." But what of those who have little or no contact with the natural world and for whom the beauties and mysteries of the earth have long since disappeared? And what of those youngsters whose lives revolve around cyberspace and technological devices and virtual images to the exclusion of anything resembling genuine nature experience? Do we not owe it to our young people to address the lessons of these essays with all the determination and strength of will we can possibly bring to bear?

ENDNOTES

1. *Generation M2: Media in the Lives of 8- to 18-Year Olds*, a national large-scale survey conducted by the Kaiser Family Foundation, was released in January 2010. This survey found that the average "screen time" for young people in America was 7 hours 38 minutes each day or 53 hours per week, a figure markedly higher than a similar study done five years earlier. The complete report can be accessed at the Kaiser website, www.kff.org.

2. A current edition of *The Sense of Wonder* is available from Harper-Collins in a splendid coffee-table format that includes Nick Kelsh's images of the Maine coastline and woodlands. The volume can be purchased through Amazon.com and is available also in Kindle format.

Richard Louv

LEAVE NO CHILD INSIDE
The growing movement to reconnect children and nature

AS A BOY, I pulled out dozens—perhaps hundreds—of survey stakes in a vain effort to slow the bulldozers that were taking out my woods to make way for a new subdivision. Had I known then what I've since learned from a developer, that I should have simply moved the stakes around to be more effective, I would surely have done that too. So you might imagine my dubiousness when, a few weeks after the publication of my 2005 book, *Last Child in the Woods*, I received an e-mail from Derek Thomas, who introduced himself as vice chairman and chief investment officer of Newland Communities, one of the nation's largest privately-owned residential development companies. "I have been reading your new book," he wrote, "and am profoundly disturbed by some of the information you present."

Thomas said he wanted to do something positive. He invited me to an envisioning session in Phoenix to "explore how Newland can improve or redefine our approach to open space preservation and the interaction between our homebuyers and nature." A few weeks later, in a conference room filled with about eighty developers, builders, and real estate marketers, I offered my sermonette. The folks in the crowd were partially responsible for the problem, I suggested, because they destroy natural habitat, design communities in ways that discourage any real contact with nature, and include covenants that virtually criminalize outdoor play—outlawing tree-climbing, fort-building, even chalk-drawing on sidewalks.

I was ready to make a fast exit when Thomas, a bearded man with an avuncular demeanor, stood up and said, "I want you all to go into small groups and solve the problem: How are we going to build communities in the future that actually connect kids with nature?" The room filled with noise and excitement. By the time the groups reassembled to report the ideas they had generated, I had glimpsed the primal power of connecting children and nature: It can inspire unexpected advocates and lure unlikely allies to enter an entirely new place. Call it the doorway effect. Once through the door, they can re-visualize seemingly intractable problems and produce solutions they might otherwise never have imagined.

A half-hour after Thomas's challenge, the groups reported their ideas. Among them: leave some land and native habitat in place (that's a good start); employ green design principles; incorporate nature trails and natural waterways; throw out the conventional covenants and restrictions that discourage or prohibit natural play and rewrite the rules to encourage it; allow kids to build forts and tree houses or plant gardens; and create small, on-site nature centers.

"Kids could become guides, using cell phones, along nature trails that lead to schools at the edge of the development," someone suggested. Were the men and women in this room just blowing smoke? Maybe. *Developers exploiting our hunger for nature*, I thought, *just as they market their subdivisions by naming their streets after the trees and streams that they destroy*. But the fact that developers, builders, and real estate marketers would approach Derek Thomas's question with such apparently heartfelt enthusiasm was revealing. The quality of their ideas mattered less than the fact that they had them. While they may not get there themselves, the people in this room were visualizing a very different future. They were undergoing a process of discovery that has proliferated around the country in the past two years, and not only among developers.

For decades, environmental educators, conservationists, and others have worked, often heroically, to bring more children to nature— usually with inadequate support from policymakers. A number of trends, including the recent unexpected national media attention to *Last Child* and "nature-deficit disorder," have now brought the concerns of these veteran advocates before a broader audience. While some may argue that the word "movement" is hyperbole, we do seem to have reached a tipping point.

State and regional campaigns, sometimes called Leave No Child Inside, have begun to form in Cincinnati, Cleveland, Chicago, the San Francisco Bay Area, St. Louis, Connecticut, Florida, Colorado, Texas, and elsewhere. A host of related initiatives—among them the simple-living, walkable-cities, nature-education, and land-trust movements—have begun to find common cause, and collective strength, through this issue. The activity has attracted a diverse assortment of people who might otherwise never work together.

In September 2006, the National Conservation Training Center and the Conservation Fund hosted the National Dialogue on Children and Nature in Shepherdstown, West Virginia. The conference drew some 350 people from around the country, representing educators, health-care experts, recreation companies, residential developers, urban planners, conservation agencies, academics, and other groups. Even the Walt Disney Company was represented. Support has also come from religious leaders, liberal and conservative, who understand that all spiritual life begins with a sense of wonder, and that one of the first windows to wonder is the natural world. "Christians should take the lead in reconnecting with nature and disconnecting from machines," writes R. Albert Mohler, Jr., president of the Southern Baptist Theological Seminary, the flagship school of the Southern Baptist Convention.

To some extent, the movement is fueled by organizational or economic self-interest. But something deeper is going on here. With its nearly universal appeal, this issue seems to hint at a more atavistic motivation. It may have something to do with what Harvard professor E.O. Wilson calls the biophilia hypothesis, which is that human beings are innately attracted to nature: Biologically, we are all still hunters and gatherers, and there is something in us, which we do not fully understand, that needs an occasional immersion in nature. We do know that when people talk about the disconnect between children and nature—if they are old enough to remember a time when outdoor play was the norm—they almost always tell stories about their own childhoods: this tree house or fort, that special woods or ditch or creek or meadow. They recall those "places of initiation," in the words of naturalist Bob Pyle, where they may have first sensed with awe and wonder the largeness of the world seen and unseen. When people share these stories, their cultural, political, and religious walls come tumbling down.

And when that happens, ideas can pour forth—and lead to ever more insightful approaches. It's a short, conceptual leap, for example, from the notions generated by Derek Thomas's working group to the creation of a truly sustainable development like the pioneering Village Homes, in Davis, California, where suburban homes are pointed inward toward open green space, vegetable gardens are encouraged, and orchards, not gates or walls, surround the community. And from there, rather than excusing more sprawl with a green patina, developers might even encourage the green redevelopment of portions of strip-mall America into Dutch-style eco-communities, where nature would be an essential strand in the fabric of the urban neighborhood.

In similar ways, the leave-no-child-inside movement could become one of the best ways to challenge other entrenched conceptions—for example, the current, test-centric definition of education reform. Bring unlike-minded people through the doorway to talk about the effect of society's nature-deficit on child development, and pretty soon they'll be asking hard questions: Just why have school districts canceled field trips and recess and environmental education? And why doesn't our school have windows that open and natural light? At a deeper level, when we challenge schools to incorporate place-based learning in the natural world, we will help students realize that school isn't supposed to be a polite form of incarceration, but a portal to the wider world.

All this may be wishful thinking, of course, at least in the short run. But as Martin Luther King, Jr., often said, the success of any social movement depends on its ability to show a world where people will want to go. The point is that thinking about children's need for nature helps us begin to paint a picture of that world—which is something that has to be done, because the price of not painting that picture is too high.

WITHIN THE SPACE of a few decades, the way children understand and experience their neighborhoods and the natural world has changed radically. Even as children and teenagers become more aware of global threats to the environment, their physical contact, their intimacy with nature, is fading. As one suburban 5th grader put it to me, in what has become the signature epigram of the children-and-nature movement: "I like to play indoors better 'cause that's where all the electrical outlets are."

His desire is not at all uncommon. In a typical week, only 6 percent of children ages nine to thirteen play outside on their own. Studies by the National Sporting Goods Association and by American Sports Data, a research firm, show a dramatic decline in the past decade in such outdoor activities as swimming and fishing. Even bike riding is down 31 percent since 1995. In San Diego, according to a survey by the nonprofit Aquatic Adventures, 90 percent of inner-city kids do not know how to swim; 34 percent have never been to the beach. In suburban Fort Collins, Colorado, teachers shake their heads in dismay when they describe the many students who have never been to the mountains visible year-round on the western horizon.

Urban, suburban, and even rural parents cite a number of everyday reasons why their children spend less time in nature than they themselves did, including disappearing access to natural areas, competition from television and computers, dangerous traffic, more homework, and other pressures. Most of all, parents cite fear of stranger-danger. Conditioned by round-the-clock news coverage, they believe in an epidemic of abductions by strangers, despite evidence that the number of child-snatchings (about a hundred a year) has remained roughly the same for two decades, and that the rates of violent crimes against young people have fallen to well below 1975 levels.

Yes, there are risks outside our homes. But there are also risks in raising children under virtual protective house arrest: threats to their independent judgment and value of place, to their ability to feel awe and wonder, to their sense of stewardship for the Earth—and, most immediately, threats to their psychological and physical health. The rapid increase in childhood obesity leads many healthcare leaders to worry that the current generation of children may be the first since World War II to die at an earlier age than their parents. Getting kids outdoors more, riding bikes, running, swimming—and, especially, experiencing nature directly— could serve as an antidote to much of what ails the young.

The physical benefits are obvious, but other benefits are more subtle and no less important. Take the development of cognitive functioning. Factoring out other variables, studies of students in California and nationwide show that schools that use outdoor classrooms and other forms of experiential education produce significant student gains in social studies, science, language arts, and math. One 2005 study by the California Department of Education found that students in outdoor science programs improved their science testing scores by 27 percent.

And the benefits go beyond test scores. According to a range of studies, children in outdoor-education settings show increases in self-esteem, problem solving, and motivation to learn. "Natural spaces and materials stimulate children's limitless imaginations," says Robin Moore, an international authority on the design of environments for children's play, learning, and education, "and serve as the medium of inventiveness and creativity." Studies of children in schoolyards with both green areas and manufactured play areas have found that children engaged in more creative forms of play in the green areas, and they also played more cooperatively. Recent research also shows a positive correlation between the length of children's attention spans and direct experience in nature. Studies at the University of Illinois show that time in natural settings significantly reduces symptoms of attention-deficit (hyperactivity) disorder in children as young as age five. The research also shows the experience helps reduce negative stress and protects psychological well-being, especially in children undergoing the most stressful life events.

Even without corroborating evidence or institutional help, many parents notice significant changes in their children's stress levels and hyperactivity when they spend time outside. "My son is still on Ritalin, but he's so much calmer in the outdoors that we're seriously considering moving to the mountains," one mother tells me. Could it simply be that he needs more physical activity? "No, he gets that, in sports," she says.

Similarly, the back page of an October issue of a San Francisco magazine displays a vivid photograph of a small boy, eyes wide with excitement and joy, leaping and running on a great expanse of California beach, storm clouds and towering waves behind him. A short article explains that the boy was hyperactive, he had been kicked out of his school, and his parents had not known what to do with him—but they had observed how nature engaged and soothed him. So for years they took their son to beaches, forests, dunes, and rivers to let nature do its work. The photograph was taken in 1907. The boy was Ansel Adams.

LAST SPRING, I FOUND MYSELF wandering down a path toward the Milwaukee River, where it runs through the urban Riverside Park. At first glance, there was nothing unusual about the young people I encountered. A group of modern inner-city high school students, they dressed in standard hip-hop fashion. I expected to see in their eyes the cynicism so fashionable now, the jaded look of what D.H. Lawrence long ago called the "know-it-all state of mind." But not today. Casting their fishing lines from the muddy bank of the Milwaukee River, they were laughing with pleasure. They were totally immersed in the fishing, delighted by the lazy, brown river and the landscape of the surrounding park, designed in the late 19th century by Frederick Law Olmsted, the founder of American landscape architecture. Ducking a few backcasts, I walked through the woods to the two-story Urban Ecology Center, made of lumber recycled from abandoned buildings.

When this Milwaukee park was established, it was a tree-lined valley, with a waterfall, a hill for sledding, and places for skating and swimming, fishing and boating. But when adjacent Riverside High School was expanded in the 1970s, some of the topography was flattened to create sports fields. Industrial and other pollution made the river unfit for human contact, park maintenance declined, and crime became a problem. Then, in the early 1990s, something remarkable happened. A retired biophysicist started a small outdoor-education program in the abandoned park. A dam on the river was removed in 1997, and natural water flow flushed out contaminants. Following a well-established pattern, crime decreased as more people used the park. Over the years, the outdoor-education program evolved into the nonprofit Urban Ecology Center, which annually hosts more than eighteen thousand student visits from twenty-three schools in the surrounding neighborhoods.

The center's director, Ken Leinbach, a former science teacher, was giving me a tour. "Many teachers would like to use outdoor classrooms, but they don't feel they're trained adequately. When the schools partner with us, they don't have to worry about training," he said. An added benefit: The center welcomes kids from the surrounding neighborhood, so they no longer associate the woods only with danger, but with joy and exploration as well. Later, we climbed to the top of a wooden tower, high above the park. Leinbach explained that the tower creates the impression that someone is watching over the kids—literally.

"From up here, I once tracked and gave phone reports to the police about a driver who was trying to hit people on the bike path," he said, looking across the treetops. "Except for that incident, no serious violent crime has occurred in the park in the past five years. We see environmental education as a great tool for urban revitalization." Even as it shows how nature can be better woven into cities, the Urban Ecology Center also helps paint a portrait of an educational future that many of us would like to see: every school connected to an outdoor classroom, as school districts partner with nature centers, nature preserves, ranches, and farms, to create the new schoolyards.

Such a future is embodied in the nature-themed schools that have begun sprouting up nationwide, like the Schlitz Audubon Nature Center Preschool, where, as the *Milwaukee Journal Sentinel* reported in April 2006, "a 3-year-old can identify a cedar tree and a maple—even if she can't tell you what color pants she's wearing. And a 4-year-old can tell the difference between squirrel and rabbit tracks—even if he can't yet read any of the writing on a map. Young children learn through the sounds, scents, and seasons of the outdoors." Taking cues from the preschool's success in engaging children, an increasing number of nature centers are looking to add preschool programs not only to meet the demand for early childhood education but also to "create outdoor enthusiasts at a young age," the *Journal Sentinel* reported. And their success points to a doorway into the larger challenge—to better care for the health of the Earth.

STUDIES SHOW THAT almost to a person conservationists or environmentalists—whatever we want to call them—had some transcendent experience in nature when they were children. For some, the epiphanies took place in a national park; for others, in the clump of trees at the end of the cul-de-sac. But if experiences in nature are radically reduced for future generations, where will stewards of the Earth come from? A few months ago, I visited Ukiah, California, a mountain town nestled in the pines and fog. Ukiah is Spotted Owl Central, a town associated with the swirling controversy regarding logging, old growth, and endangered species. This is one of the most bucolic landscapes in our country, but local educators and parents report that Ukiah kids aren't going outside much anymore. So who will care about the spotted owl in ten or fifteen years?

Federal and state conservation agencies are asking such questions with particular urgency. The reason: Though the roads at some U.S. national parks remain clogged, overall visits by Americans have dropped by 25 percent since 1987, few people get far from their cars, and camping is on the decline. And such trends may further reduce political support for parks. In October 2006, the superintendent of Yellowstone National Park joined the cadre of activists around the country calling for a no-child-left-inside campaign to make children more comfortable with the outdoors. In a similar move, the U.S. Forest Service is launching More Kids in the Woods, which would fund local efforts to get children outdoors.

Nonprofit environmental organizations are also showing a growing interest in how children engage with nature. In early 2006, the Sierra Club intensified its commitment to connecting children to nature through its Inner City Outings program for at-risk youths, and it has ramped up its legislative efforts in support of environmental education. The National Wildlife Federation is rolling out the Green Hour, a national campaign to persuade parents to encourage their children to spend one hour a day in nature. John Flicker, president of the National Audubon Society, is campaigning for the creation of a family-focused nature center in every congressional district in the nation. "Once these centers are embedded, they're almost impossible to kill," says Flicker. "They help create a political constituency right now, but also build a future political base for conservation."

Proponents of a new San Diego Regional Canyonlands Park, which would protect the city's unique web of urban canyons, have adjusted their efforts to address these younger constituents. "In addition to the other arguments to do this, such as protecting wildlife," says Eric Bowlby, Sierra Club Canyons Campaign coordinator, "we've been talking about the health and educational benefits of these canyons to kids. People who may not care about endangered species do care about their kids' health." For conservationists, it could be a small step from initiatives like these to the idea of dedicating a portion of any proposed open space to children and families in the surrounding area. The acreage could include nature centers, which ideally would provide outdoor-oriented preschools and other offerings. Of course, such programs must teach children how to step lightly on natural habitats, especially ones with endangered species. But the outdoor experiences of children are essential for the survival of conservation. And so the truth is that the human child in nature may be the most important indicator species of future sustainability.

The future of children in nature has profound implications not only for the conservation of land but also for the direction of the environmental movement. If society embraces something as simple as the health benefits of nature experiences for children, it may begin to re-evaluate the worth of "the environment." While public-health experts have traditionally associated environmental health with the absence of toxic pollution, the definition fails to account for an equally valid consideration: how the environment can *improve* human health. Seen through that doorway, nature isn't a problem, it's the solution: Environmentalism is essential to our own well-being. Howard Frumkin, director of the National Center for Environmental Health, points out that future research about the positive health effects of nature should be conducted in collaboration with architects, urban planners, park designers, and landscape architects. "Perhaps we will advise patients to take a few days in the country, to spend time gardening," he wrote in a 2001 *American Journal of Preventive Medicine* article, "or [we will] build hospitals in scenic locations, or plant gardens in rehabilitation centers. Perhaps the ... organizations that pay for health care will come to fund such interventions, especially if they prove to rival pharmaceuticals in cost and efficacy."

Here's one suggestion for how to accelerate that change, starting with children: Nationally and internationally, pediatricians and other health professionals could use office posters, pamphlets, and personal persuasion to promote the physical and mental health benefits of nature play. Such publicity would give added muscle to efforts to reduce child obesity. Ideally, health providers would add nature therapy to the traditional approaches to attention-deficit disorders and childhood depression. This effort might be modeled on the national physical-fitness campaign launched by President John F. Kennedy. We could call the campaign "Grow Outside!"

IN EVERY ARENA, from conservation and health to urban design and education, a growing children-and-nature movement will have no shortage of tools to bring about a world in which we leave no child inside—and no shortage of potential far-reaching benefits. Under the right conditions, cultural and political change can occur rapidly. The recycling and antismoking campaigns are our best examples of how social and political pressure can work hand-in-hand to create a societal transformation in just one generation. The children-and-nature movement has perhaps even greater potential—because it touches something even deeper within us, biologically and spiritually.

In January 2005, I attended a meeting of the Quivira Coalition, a New Mexico organization that brings together ranchers and environmentalists to find common ground. The coalition is now working on a plan to promote ranches as the new schoolyards. When my turn came to speak, I told the audience how, when I was a boy, I pulled out all those survey stakes in an attempt to keep the earthmovers at bay. Afterward, a rancher stood up. He was wearing scuffed boots. His aged jeans had never seen acid wash, only dirt and rock. His face was sunburned and creased. His drooping moustache was white, and he wore thick eyeglasses with heavy plastic frames, stained with sweat. "You know that story you told about pulling up stakes?" he said. "I did that when I was a boy, too."

The crowd laughed. I laughed.

And then the man began to cry. Despite his embarrassment, he continued to speak, describing the source of his sudden grief: that he might belong to one of the last generations of Americans to feel that sense of ownership of land and nature. The power of this movement lies in that sense, that special place in our hearts, those woods where the bulldozers cannot reach. Developers and environmentalists, corporate CEOs and college professors, rock stars and ranchers may agree on little else, but they agree on this: No one among us wants to be a member of the last generation to pass on to its children the joy of playing outside in nature.

Lowell Monke

THE HUMAN TOUCH

In the rush to place a computer on every desk, schools are neglecting intellectual creativity and personal growth.

IN 1922 THOMAS EDISON proclaimed, "I believe the motion picture is destined to revolutionize our educational system and that in a few years it will supplant largely, if not entirely, the use of textbooks." Thus began a long string of spectacularly wrong predictions regarding the capacity of various technologies to revolutionize education.

What betrayed Edison and his successors was an uncritical faith in technology itself. This faith has become a sort of ideology increasingly dominating K–12 education. In the past two decades, school systems, with generous financial and moral support from foundations and all levels of government, have made massive investments in computer technology and in creating "wired" schools. The goal is twofold: to provide children with the computer skills necessary to flourish in a high-tech world and to give them access to tools and information that will enhance their learning in subjects such as mathematics and history.

However, in recent years a number of scholars have questioned the vast sums being devoted to educational technology. They rarely quibble with the need for children to learn how to use computers, but find little evidence that making technology more available leads to higher student achievement in core subjects. As Stanford University professor Larry Cuban writes in *Oversold and Underused*, "There have been no advances (measured by higher academic achievement of urban, suburban or rural students) over the past decade that can be confidently attributed to broader

28

access to computers. ... The link between test-score improvements and computer availability and use is even more contested."

While it is important to examine the relationship between technology and learning, that debate often devolves into a tit-for-tat of dueling studies and anecdotes. The problem with framing the issue merely as a question of whether technology boosts test scores is that it fails to address the interaction between technology and the values learned in school. In short, we need to ask what kind of learning tends to take place with the computer and what kind gets left out.

The Need for Firsthand Experience

A computer can inundate a child with mountains of information. However, all of this learning takes place the same way: through abstract symbols, decontextualized and cast onto a two-dimensional screen. Contrast that with the way children come to know a tree—by peeling its bark, climbing its branches, sitting under its shade, jumping into its piled-up leaves. Just as important, these firsthand experiences are enveloped by feelings and associations—muscles being used, sun warming the skin, blossoms scenting the air. The computer cannot even approximate any of this.

There is a huge qualitative difference between learning about something, which requires only information, and learning from something, which requires that the learner enter into a rich and complex relationship with the subject at hand. For younger children especially, that relationship is as physical as it is mental. Rousseau pointed out long ago that the child's first and most important teacher is his hands. Every time I walk through a store with my sons and grow tired of saying, "Don't touch that!" I am reminded of Rousseau's wisdom.

What "Information Age" values tempt us to forget is that all of the information gushing through our electronic networks is abstract; that is, it is all representations, one or more symbolic steps removed from any concrete object or personal experience. Abstract information must somehow connect to a child's concrete experiences if it is to be meaningful. If there is little personal, concrete experience with which to connect, those abstractions become inert bits of data, unlikely to mobilize genuine interest or to generate comprehension of the objects and ideas they represent. Furthermore, making meaning of new experiences—and the ideas that grow out of them—requires quiet contemplation. By pumping information at children at phenomenal speed, the computer short-circuits that process. As social critic Theodore Roszak states in *The Cult of Information*, "An excess of information may actually crowd out ideas, leaving the mind (young minds especially) distracted by sterile, disconnected facts, lost among the shapeless heaps of data."

This deluge of shapeless heaps of data caused the late social critic Marshall McLuhan to conclude that schools would have to become "recognized as civil defense against media fallout." McLuhan understood that the consumption and manipulation of symbolic, abstract information is not an adequate substitute for concrete, firsthand involvement with objects, people, nature and community, for it ignores the child's primary educational need—to make meaning out of experience.

Simulation's Limits

Of course computers can simulate experience. However, one of the byproducts of these simulations is the replacement of values inherent in real experience with a different set of abstract values that are compatible with the technological ideology. For example, "Oregon Trail," a computer game that helps children simulate the exploration of the American frontier, teaches students that the pioneers' success in crossing the Great Plains depended most decisively on managing their resources. This is the message implicit in the game's structure, which asks students, in order to survive, to make a series of rational, calculated decisions based on precise measurements of their resources. In other words, good pioneers were good accountants.

But this completely misses the deeper significance of this great American migration, which lies not in the computational capabilities of the pioneers but in their determination, courage, ingenuity, and faith as they overcame extreme conditions and their almost constant miscalculations.

Because the computer cannot traffic in these deeply human qualities, the resilient souls of the pioneers are absent from the simulation.

Here we encounter the ambiguity of technology: its propensity to promote certain qualities while sidelining others. McLuhan called this process amplification and amputation. He used the microphone as an example. The microphone can literally amplify one's voice, but in doing so it reduces the speaker's need to exercise his own lung power. Thus one's inner capacities may atrophy.

This phenomenon is of particular concern with children, who are in the process of developing all kinds of inner capacities. Examples abound of technology's circumventing the developmental process: the student who uses a spell checker instead of learning to spell, the student who uses a calculator instead of learning to add—young people sacrificing internal growth for external power.

Often, however, this process is not so easily identified. An example is the widespread use of computers in preschools and elementary schools to improve sagging literacy skills. What could be wrong with that? Quite a bit, if we consider the prerequisites to reading and writing. We know that face-to-face conversation is a crucial element in the development of both oral and written communication skills. On the one hand, conversation forces children to generate their own images, which provide connections to the language they hear and eventually will read. This is one reason why reading to children and telling them stories is so important. Television and computers, on the other hand, generally require nothing more than the passive acceptance of prefabricated images.

Now consider that a study reported in *U.S. News & World Report* estimated that the current generation of children, with its legions of struggling readers, would experience one-third fewer face-to-face conversations during their school years than the generation of 30 years ago. It may well be that educators are trying to solve the problem of illiteracy by turning to the very technology that has diminished the very experiences children need to become literate.

Obsolete Lessons

But students need to start using computers early in order to prepare for the high-tech future, don't they? Consider that the vast majority of students graduating from college this past spring started kindergarten in 1986, two years after Macintosh was invented. If they used computers at all in elementary school, they were probably command-line machines with no mouse, no hard drive, and only rudimentary graphics. By the time these students graduated from college, whatever computer skills they picked up in primary school had long been rendered obsolete by the frenetic pace of technological innovation.

The general computer skills a youth needs to enter the workplace or college can easily be learned in one year of instruction during high school. During the nine years that I taught Advanced Computer Technology for the Des Moines public schools, I discovered that the level of computer skills students brought to the class had little bearing on their success. Teaching them the computer skills was the easy part. What I was not able to provide were the rich and varied firsthand experiences students needed in order to connect the abstract symbols they had to manipulate on the screen to the world around them. Students with scant computer experience but rich ideas and life experiences were, by the end of the year, generating sophisticated relational databases, designing marketable websites, and creating music videos. Ironically, it was the students who had curtailed their time climbing the trees, rolling the dough, and conversing with friends and adults in order to become computer "wizards" who typically had the most trouble finding creative things to do with the computer.

Certainly, many of these highly skilled young people (almost exclusively young men) find opportunities to work on computer and software design at prestigious universities and corporations. But such jobs represent a minuscule percentage of the occupations in this nation. And in any case, the task of early education is not merely to prepare students for making a living; it is to help them learn how to make a life. For that purpose, the computer wizards in my class seemed particularly ill-prepared.

So why is it that schools persist in believing they must expose children to computers early? I think it is for the same reason that we take our children to church, to Fourth of July parades, and indeed to rituals of all types: to initiate them into a culture—in this case, the culture of high technology. The purpose is to infuse them with a set of values that supports the high-tech culture that has spread so rapidly across our society. And this, as we shall see, is perhaps the most disturbing trend of all.

The Ecological Impact of Technology

As the promise of a computer revolution in education fades, I often hear promoters fall back on what I'll term the neutrality argument: "Computers are just tools; it's what you do with them that matters." In some sense this is no more than a tautology: Of course it matters how we use computers in schools. What matters more, however, is that we use them at all. Every tool demands that we somehow change our environment or values in order to accommodate its use. For instance, the building of highways to accommodate the automobile hastened the flight to the suburbs and the decline of inner cities. And over the past 50 years we have radically altered our social landscape to accommodate the television set. In his seminal book *Autonomous Technology*, Langdon Winner dubbed this characteristic "reverse adaptation."

Consider the school personnel who already understand, intuitively, how this principle works: the music teacher whose program has been cut in order to fund computer labs, the principal who has had to beef up security in order to protect high-priced technology, the superintendent who has had to craft an "acceptable use" agreement that governs children's use of the Internet (and for the first time in our history renounces the school's responsibility for the material children are exposed to while in school). What the computers-are-just-tools argument ignores is the ecological nature of powerful technologies—that is, their introduction into an environment reconstitutes all of the relationships in that environment, some for better and some for worse. Clinging to the belief that computers have no effect on us allows us to turn a blind eye to the sacrifices that schools have made to accommodate them.

Not only do computers send structural ripples throughout a school system, but they also subtly alter the way we think about education. The old saw, "To a man with a hammer everything looks like a nail," has many corollaries. (The walls of my home once testified to one of my favorites: To a 4-year-old with a crayon, everything looks like drawing paper.) One that fits here is: "To an educator with a computer, everything looks like information." And the more prominent we make computers in schools (and in our own lives), the more we see the rapid accumulation, manipulation, and sharing of information as central to the learning process—edging out the contemplation and expression of ideas and the gradual development of meaningful connections to the world.

In reconstituting learning as the acquisition of information, the computer also shifts our values. The computer embodies a particular value system, a technological thought world first articulated by Francis Bacon and Rene Descartes four hundred years ago, that turns our attention outward toward asserting control over our environment (that is essentially what technologies do—extend our power to control from a distance). As it has gradually come to dominate Western thinking, this ideology has entered our educational institutions. Its growing dominance is witnessed in the language that abounds in education: talk of empowerment, student control of learning, standards, assessment tools, and productivity. Almost gone from the conversation are those inner concerns—wisdom, truth, character, imagination, creativity, and meaning—that once formed the core values of education. Outcomes have replaced insights as the yardstick of learning, while standardized tests are replacing human judgment as the means of assessment. No tool supports this technological shift more than computers.

In the Wrong Hands

There are some grave consequences in pushing technological values too far and too soon. Soon after my high school computer lab was hooked up to the Internet, I realized that my students suddenly had more power to do more damage to more people than any teenagers in history. Had they been carefully prepared to assume responsibility for that power through the arduous process of developing self-discipline, ethical and moral strength, compassion, and connection with the community around them? Hardly. They and their teachers had been too busy putting that power to use.

We must help our young people develop the considerable moral and ethical strength needed to resist abusing the enormous power these machines give them. Those qualities take a great deal of time and effort to develop in a child, but they ought to be as much a prerequisite to using powerful computer tools as is learning how to type. Trying to teach a student to use the power of computer technology appropriately without those moral and ethical traits is like trying to grow a tree without roots. Rather than nurture those roots, we hand our youngest children machines and then gush about the power and control they display over that rarefied environment. From the earliest years we teach our children that if they have a problem, we have an external tool that will fix it. (Computers are not the only tools. Ritalin, for example, is a powerful technology that has been scandalously overprescribed to "fix" behavior problems.) After years of this training, when our teenagers find themselves confused, angry, depressed, or overwhelmed, we wonder why so many of them don't reach out to the community for help or dig deep within themselves to find the internal strength to persevere, but rather reach for the most powerful (and often deadly) tool they can find to "fix" their problems. Our attempts to use powerful machines to accelerate or remediate learning are part of a pattern that sacrifices the growth of our children's inner resources and deep connectedness to community for the ability to extend their power outward into the world. The world pays a high price for the trade-off.

The response that I often hear to this criticism—that we just need to balance computer use in school with more "hands-on" activities (and maybe a little character education)—sounds reasonable. Certainly, schools should help young people develop balanced lives. But the call for balance within schools ignores the massive commitment of resources required to make computers work at all and the resultant need to keep them constantly in use to justify that expense. Furthermore, that view of balance completely discounts the enormous imbalance of children's lives outside of school.

Children typically spend nearly half their waking life outside of school sitting in front of screens. Their world is saturated with the artificial, the abstract, the mechanical. Whereas the intellectual focus of schools in the rural society of the 19th century compensated for a childhood steeped in nature and concrete activity, balance today requires a reversal of roles, with schools compensating for the overly abstract, symbolic, and artificial environment that children experience outside of school.

Technology with a Human Purpose

None of this is to say that we should banish computers from all levels of K–12 education. As young people move into subject areas such as advanced mathematics and chemistry that rely on highly abstract concepts, computers have much to offer. Young people will also need computer skills when they graduate. But computer-based learning needs to grow out of years of concrete experience and a fundamental appreciation for the world apart from the machine, a world in which nature and human beings are able to speak for and through themselves to the child. Experiences with the computer need to grow out of early reliance on simple tools that depend on and develop the skills of the child rather than complex tools, which have so many skills already built in. By concentrating high technology in the upper grades, we honor the natural developmental stages of childhood. And there is a bonus: the release of massive amounts of resources currently tied up in expensive machinery that can be redirected toward helping young children develop the inner resources needed to put that machinery to good use when they become adults.

There remains a problem, however. When Bacon began pushing the technological ideology, Western civilization was full of meaning and wretchedly short on the material means of survival. Today we face the reverse situation: a society saturated in material comforts but almost devoid of meaning. Schools that see their job as preparing young people to meet the demands of a technology-driven world merely embrace and advance the idea that human needs are no longer our highest priority, that we must adapt to meet the demands of our machines. We may deliver our children into the world with tremendous technical power, but it is rarely with a well-developed sense of human purpose to guide its use.

If we are to alter that relationship, we will have to think of technological literacy in a new way. Perhaps we could call it technology awareness. Whatever its name, that kind of study, rather than technology training, is what needs to be integrated into the school curriculum. I am currently working with the Alliance for Childhood on a set of developmental guidelines to help educators create technology-awareness programs that help young people think about, not just work with, technology. This is not the place to go into the details of those guidelines. What I want to emphasize here is that they share one fundamental feature: They situate technology within a set of human values rather than out in front of those values. They do not start by asking what children need to do to adapt to a machine world, but rather, which technologies can best serve human purposes at every educational level and how we can prepare children to make wise decisions about their use in the future.

The most daunting problems facing our society—drugs, violence, racism, poverty, the dissolution of family and community, and certainly war—are all matters of human purpose and meaning. Filling schools with computers will not help find the answers to why the freest nation in the world has the highest percentage of citizens behind bars or why the wealthiest nation in history condemns a sixth of its children to poverty.

So it seems that we are faced with a remarkable irony: That in an age of increasing artificiality, children first need to sink their hands deeply into what is real; that in an age of light-speed communication, it is crucial that children take the time to develop their own inner voice; that in an age of incredibly powerful machines, we must first teach our children how to use the incredible powers that lie deep within themselves.

David Sobel

LOOK, DON'T TOUCH
The problem with environmental education

THE KIDS HAVE BEEN UP since 7:30 playing computer games and watching cartoons. *What a travesty for them to be inside on such a beautiful day*, you harrumph to yourself. On the refrigerator, you notice the schedule of events from the nearby nature center. "Let's Get Face to Face with Flowers," it beckons. *Just the thing!* It's a sparkly May morning. Buds are bursting. There's a warm breeze full of the aromatic scent of the woods just waking up.

You trundle the kids into the minivan. They despondently consent. "Do we have to do a program? Programs are boring," the older one complains. But as soon as you pull into the parking lot at Happy Hills Nature Center, their faces brighten. They fling the sliding door open and scamper down through the blossom-filled meadow to the shore of the pond. Ross, age seven, pulls off his sneakers and wades in, bent over searching for frogs. Amanda, age ten, plops down and starts making a dandelion tiara. *What a good decision*, you think to yourself.

Terri, the smiley naturalist wearing the official Happy Hills insigniaed staff shirt, saunters over. "Here for the flower program?" she chirps. "We're meeting up in the Cozy Corner room to get started."

Ross asks, "Can Freddie come too?" holding up the fat, green frog he has befriended.

Terri's bright face darkens a bit. "Sorry. Freddie needs to stay in the pond. Did you know the oils from your hands can make Freddie sick?"

In the darkened Cozy Corner room, Terri has prepared a PowerPoint of all the flowers you might see on the trail today. "Here are some spring

38

beauties. They look just like little peppermint candies. But, of course, we can't eat them. And here's one of my favorites, Dutchman's breeches. Why do you think we call them that?"

After about the seventh slide the kids start to squirm in their seats. "Daddy, I have to go pee," complains Ross. After about the twenty-seventh slide, you too have to go pee.

"And now, let's see how many we can find," Terri says. It's good to be back outside. Upon entering the woods, Amanda notices a red eft in a patch of moss. She takes a few steps off the trail and Terri chastises her: "Remember, Amanda, nature is fragile! When you walk off the trail, you crush all kinds of little creatures you can't see." Farther on Ross scampers up into the inviting branches of a tree that has fallen across the trail. "Sorry, Ross, no climbing, too dangerous, we wouldn't want you to get hurt." At each flower, Terri circles everyone around and tells them the Latin name, the herbal uses, the pollinator, the … . Once in a while someone gets to touch the petals, only *veeerrry* gently. Picking flowers is strictly verboten.

Toward the end of the walk, the trail comes out by the pond, where Amanda finds her discarded dandelion tiara and slips it into her shirt, watching to make sure Terri doesn't notice. On the ride home, no one talks.

"Well, that was fun," you enthuse, trying to get the conversation going.

Amanda extracts her dandelion tiara and perches it on her head. "Picking flowers was fun. But we told you about programs, Daddy. Too many rules. It would've been fun if we could have just played all together in the meadow." You find that you agree.

Contrast this experience with John Muir's recollection of arriving at his family's first American homestead in remote Fountain Lake, Wisconsin, when he was eleven. Within minutes, he and his brother were up in a tree observing a blue jay's nest. From there they raced about to find a bluebird's nest, then a woodpecker's, and thus "began an acquaintance with the frogs and snakes and turtles in the creeks and springs." The new world of untamed America was thrilling for John and his brother:

The sudden plash into pure wildness—baptism in Nature's warm heart—how utterly happy it made us! Nature streaming into us, wooingly teaching her wonderful glowing lessons, so unlike the dismal grammar ashes and cinders so long thrashed into us. ...Young hearts, young leaves, flowers, animals, the winds and the streams and the sparkling lake, all wildly, gladly rejoicing together!

This is the joy of children encountering the natural world on their own terms, and more and more it is becoming a lost idyll, no longer an integral part of growing up. There are many reasons for this loss—urbanization, the changing social structure of families, tick- and mosquito-borne illnesses, the fear of stranger-danger. And perhaps even environmental education is one of the causes of children's alienation from nature.

I know that's a puzzling statement. You're thinking: Environmental education is supposed to connect children with nature, to get them started on a lifetime of loving and wanting to protect the natural world. Yes— that's what is supposed to happen. But somewhere along the way, much of environmental education has lost its magic, its "wildly, gladly rejoicing together." Instead, it's become didactic and staid, restrictive and rule-bound. A creeping focus on cognition has replaced the goal of exhilaration that once motivated educators to take children outside.

Much of environmental education today has taken on a museum mentality, where nature is a composed exhibit on the other side of the glass. Children can look at it and study it, but they can't do anything with it. The message is: *Nature is fragile. Look, but don't touch.* Ironically, this "take only photographs, leave only footprints" mindset crops up in the policies and programs of many organizations trying to preserve the natural world and cultivate children's relationships to it.

IF YOU WALK THE driftwood-cluttered shores along Maine's crenulated coast, you'll find a number of ramshackle constructions in the coves. KID'S FORT! NO ADULTS ALLOWED! a hand-lettered sign will warn. The forts are woven into the spruce blowdown at the edge of the shore, or crouched between the top of the beach cobble and the steep, blackberried bank. Planks, lobster pots, buoys, scrap metal, broken ladders, discarded tarps are pieced together to create bedrooms, lookouts, kitchens, storage cabinets. It is clear that deep, unadulterated play is alive in these salty edges beyond the purview of parents. And yet, on many land trust properties on the coast of Maine, fort-building is outlawed because of concerns over liability and unsightliness.

I believe that the imaginative, constructive practice of fort-building actually fosters the sense of connectedness that land trusts want to cultivate in young people. It's an instinctive drive to make a home in the world away from the home your parents provided you. When you make a fort, or den, or hideout, it creates a connection to the land, nurturing an affinity for that place. Discouraging these natural tendencies of childhood could actually lead to resentment of, and a lack of commitment to, the land trust's agenda of land preservation. When I wrote an op-ed piece for the *Bangor Daily News* articulating this conviction, one Maine land trust board member responded:

> Realistically, if the land trust allowed some fort-building along the shore, then how much is too much? Following typical monkey-see, monkey-do behavior, if one fort is built, then other people come along and decide to build a second fort, and so it goes. Then we've got a neighborhood of forts that has become a distraction and an eyesore to those who want to teach kids to appreciate nature using a light-handed approach. The scale of fairy house construction on another coastal island is testimony to the scourge this can become.

See what I mean?

Head south to Texas and you'll encounter more of the same. At the Lady Bird Johnson Wildflower Center in Austin, the trails ramble through hill country chaparral—hardy shrubs, some cactus, copses of woods. It's an unfragile, wonderfully explorable landscape. When I asked if children were allowed to go off the trails, to play in the little pockets of woods, the education director looked at me disapprovingly. "Oh no, we can't let children do that." The intimation was that this was way too dangerous for the children and would have too much impact on the natural resource. I wasn't convinced that either of these concerns was well-founded or based on data.

It's true in the inner city as well. When a friend of mine was the education director at the Arnold Arboretum in Boston, she was trying to create programs that encouraged the multiethnic children who lived in the neighborhood to develop a love for trees. When I asked, "Well, do you let children climb any of the trees?" I got the same disapproving look from her. Tree climbing? Just not possible. Sure, I agree that the rare trees in the arboretum should be off-limits, but the big, spreading native maples and beeches, the hemlocks down along the stream—why not? Children have been climbing trees for millennia; it's great exercise, and in the vast majority of cases, they don't get hurt. Keep in mind that children get hurt from falls in the bathtub, and we don't prohibit showers. Similarly, children get injured playing competitive sports. We tolerate the risk of injury from field hockey and soccer because we value the physical and social benefits. Why don't we have the same risk/benefit mindset in relation to climbing trees?

Between the ages of six and twelve, children have an innate desire to explore the woods, build forts, make potions from wild berries, dig to China, and each of these activities is an organic, natural way for them to develop environmental values and behaviors. Instead, the "look but don't touch" approach cuts kids off from nature, teaching them that nature is boring and fraught with danger. Inadvertently, these messages send children back inside to the dynamic interactivity of computer games. Could it be that our fear of litigation and our puritanical concerns for protecting each and every blade of grass are hampering the development of the very stewardship values and behaviors that we environmental educators all say we're trying to foster? I believe so.

As a child in his native Scotland, John Muir vigorously embraced the natural world, having described himself as "a devout martyr of wildness"—a wild child. He was also a courageous inventor.

> We made guns out of gas-pipe, mounted them on sticks of any shape, clubbed our pennies together for powder, gleaned pieces of lead here and there and cut them into slugs, and, while one aimed, another applied a match to the touch-hole. With these awful weapons we wandered along the beach and fired at the gulls and solan-geese as they passed us. Fortunately we never hurt any of them that we knew of. We also dug holes in the ground, put in a handful or two of powder, tamped it well around a fuse made of a wheat-stalk, and, reaching cautiously forward, touched a match to the straw. This we called making earthquakes. Oftentimes we went home with singed hair and faces well peppered with powder-grains that could not be washed out.

This is probably not the kind of boy you'd want your children out roaming the neighborhood with. Dangerous, unmannered, destructive perhaps. Certainly, you've never seen an "Inventing Guns and Shooting Sea Gulls" program on Saturday mornings at the nature center. And yet John Muir helped create the national park system, and his writing has fostered environmental values and behaviors in countless millions of people. My contention is that John Muir's preservationist instincts grew in part out of these childhood experiences, which probably contributed more to his commitment to the natural world than learning the difference between sedimentary, metamorphic, and igneous rocks in the mandated 3rd grade curriculum.

Or consider how Harvard entomologist and biodiversity advocate E.O. Wilson describes some of his early formative experiences in nature:

> I hunted reptiles: stunned and captured five-lined skinks with a slingshot, and learned the correct maneuver for catching

Carolina anole lizards (approach, let them scuttle to the other side of the tree trunk and out of sight, peek to see where they are sitting, then take them by grabbing blind with one hand around the trunk). One late afternoon I brought home a coachwhip snake nearly as long as I was tall and walked into the house with it wrapped around my neck.

Wilson, Muir, Rachel Carson, and Aldo Leopold all had such down-and-dirty experiences in childhood. Wilson didn't just look at butterflies, he collected them. He didn't take only photographs and leave only footprints, he caught ants and put them in jars to observe them. He was a collector, not a photographer, and he was allowed to indulge his curiosity without the scolding finger of an interfering adult. Generalizing from his own biographic experience, he summarizes, "Hands-on experience at the critical time, not systematic knowledge, is what counts in the making of a naturalist. Better to be an untutored savage for a while, not to know the names or anatomical detail. Better to spend long stretches of time just searching and dreaming."

Herein lie my two main points. First, environmental educators need to allow children to be "untutored savages" for a while. Nature programs should invite children to make mud pies, climb trees, catch frogs, paint their faces with charcoal, get their hands dirty and their feet wet. They should be allowed to go off the trail and have fun. Second, environmental educators need to focus way more on hands-on experience with children and way less on systematic knowledge. Or at least understand that systematic knowledge can emerge organically from lots of hands-on experience. Between the ages of six and twelve, learning about nature is less important than simply getting children out into nature.

Terri, the Happy Hills naturalist, could have started the flower program right there in the meadow, having everyone make dandelion chains. (Call it "Removing Invasives" if you must.) She could have chosen three flowers to focus on that morning and challenged the children to learn to identify them blindfolded, by scent only. She might have had the children crawl through the meadow to see flowers at woodchuck level or given them dead bees on probes and challenged them to collect pollen from flowers with different structures. Out of these wild experiences, some systematic knowledge would have emerged. And Amanda and Ross might have said, "Wow, I never knew flowers were so cool!"

THINGS STARTED OUT DIFFERENTLY for environmental education. The summer camp movement, one of the precursors of nature and environmental education, emerged at the turn of the 20th century and was founded on the principle of embracing the vigorous outdoors life. One of its proponents, Dr. Eugene Swan, was the founder of Pine Island Camp, a preeminent Maine camp for boys. He wrote, "It will do you more good ... to sleep under boughs aslant, by a mountain lake with the trout broiling, than to see the Congressional Library or Niagara Falls." And he believed that the "heeding of Nature's ever-calling voice, and an adaptation of our lives to her laws, is going to become a salvation of the American race." Swan advocated for the character-forming benefits of early morning plunges in the lake, living off the land, sleeping under the stars, midnight rituals, and complex fantastical games. He considered his camp to be "the village of Boyville," where campers could be swept up by the "great adventure into the magic land of boyhood." Similar adventures in Girlville soon followed.

He and his camp directors created the War Game, the Whitehead Game, and a raft of other large, complex landscape games that take place over hours or days and challenged boys to run long distances in the woods, creep secretively, detect subtle clues, endure swarms of mosquitoes, behave valiantly and heroically. Campers were immersed in, at one with, and consumed by nature. They forded rivers, ate fish they caught and berries they collected, tromped through swamps, climbed trees, constructed forts, followed tracks, captured snakes, did all the things that John Muir, Rachel Carson, Aldo Leopold, and most of the other great naturalists did in their childhoods.

The Boy and Girl Scouts movements emerged not long after. The emphasis here was on primitive living skills—camping in the wilderness, building fires, making bows and arrows, preparing hides, tracking animals. In their original forms, these movements honored the deep inner desire in middle childhood to be self-sufficient, to learn how to survive with nothing but a jackknife and some strands of rawhide. The persistent popularity even today of Jean Craighead George's books—such as *My Side of the Mountain* and *Julie of the Wolves*—suggests that these instincts still persist. The rage over Suzanne Collins's *The Hunger Games* springs forth from this same deep well. These desires are encoded in our genes, compelling children to connect with their wild selves.

From the summer camp and Scouting roots, the environmental education movement emerged in the late 1960s and '70s. It started out as nature education, but with all the bad news about rainforest destruction, the ozone hole, and toxics in the environment, it soon became dominated by a desire to recruit children to fix all these problems. The tendency to push things down onto developmentally unsuspecting young children, like the pressure to learn to read in kindergarten, led to the creation of a generation of children fearful of the death of the planet at the hands of uncaring humans. A UNESCO definition from the late '70s says that "environmental education ... should prepare the individual for life through an understanding of the *major problems* [emphasis mine] of the contemporary world, and the provision of skills and attributes needed to play a productive role towards improving life and protecting the environment."

Meanwhile, in formal educational spheres, environmental education wanted to play with the big boys. It wanted to be more like reading and math and science, wanted to be more incorporated into the academic standards. As a result, environmental education got reduced to a set of facts to be mastered, content to be internalized and regurgitated. In the efforts to gain legitimacy and solve pressing problems, all the joy was sucked out of environmental education.

THE BIG QUESTION IS: What's the most effective way to parent and educate children so that they will grow up to behave in environmentally responsible ways? Or, more specifically, what kinds of learning, or what kinds of experience, will most likely shape young adults who want to protect the environment, serve on conservation commissions, think about the implications of their consumer decisions, and minimize the environmental footprints of their personal lives and the organizations where they work? Interestingly, there's an emergent body of research that's starting to clarify the relationship between childhood experience and adult stewardship behavior.

First, a number of researchers surveyed environmentalists to determine if there were any similarities in their childhood experiences that might have led to their having strong ecological values or their choice of an environmental career. When Louise Chawla of the University of Colorado reviewed these studies, she found a striking pattern. Most environmentalists attributed their commitment to a combination of two sources: "many hours spent outdoors in a keenly remembered wild or semi-wild place in childhood or adolescence and an adult who taught respect for nature." Involvement with organizations like Scouts or environmental clubs was cited by significantly fewer of the respondents. Chawla found that environmentalists talk about free play and exploration in nature and family members who focused their attention on plants or animal behavior. They don't talk much about formal education and informal nature education. Only in late childhood and adolescence do summer camp, teachers, and environmental clubs start to show up as being contributors to the individual's environmental values and behaviors. It seems that allowing children to be "untutored savages" early on can lead to environmental knowledge in due time.

Some researchers then said: Well, let's not only look at environmentalists. How about the general public, Joe the plumber? What affects whether they develop environmental attitudes and behaviors? Nancy Wells and Kristi Lekies from Cornell University took on this question and described their findings in "Nature and the Life Course: Pathways from Childhood Nature Experiences to Adult Environmentalism." The study is based on interviews with two thousand adults (plumbers, teachers, accountants, nurses, policemen) ranging in age from eighteen to ninety, chosen randomly from more than one hundred urban areas around the country. The researchers compared three kinds of childhood nature experience—wild nature experience, domesticated nature experience, and environmental education. They found that "childhood participation in 'wild' nature, such as hiking or playing in the woods, camping, and hunting or fishing, as well as participation with 'domesticated' nature such as picking flowers or produce, planting trees or seeds, and caring for plants in childhood have a positive relationship to adult environmental values. 'Wild nature' participation is also positively associated with environmental behaviors in adulthood."

Let me translate and elaborate. They found that wild nature experience in childhood correlates with adult environmental values and behavior. Domesticated nature experience correlates with adult environmental values but not so much with behavior. Perhaps most surprising, the study found that "participation in environmental education programs (in school, in Scouts, at camp, or in community environmental improvement programs) was not a significant predictor of either environmental attitudes or behaviors."

Uh-oh! The whole environmental education community kind of flinched when this finding surfaced. But the researchers were quick to say that their surveys weren't really fine grained enough to differentiate between environmental education experiences that were didactic and distancing versus those that were more hands-on, exploratory, and encouraging of that kind of wild nature play that happens in Boyville. Either way, the take-away message remains the same: There's something valuable in letting children wildly, gladly rejoice together. Catching frogs, making dandelion chains, gamboling through the meadows, playing Sally the Salamander all play a role in encouraging children to grow up into adults who recycle.

Jim Pease at Iowa State extended the investigation into the heartland, where he looked at this same relationship between childhood experiences and adult environmental stewardship behavior in farmers. He decided that he'd focus his study on farmers who took advantage of wetlands set-aside funding, which provides funding to farmers who voluntarily set aside some of their acreage from crop production and allow it to be used by migrating waterfowl. Essentially, they're taking a reduction in income in order to help wildlife. He identified 300 similar Iowa farmers, 150 who took advantage of wetlands set-aside funding and 150 who didn't. Then he did comprehensive interviews and questionnaires with all of them about their childhood experiences. He found that the farmers who displayed stewardship behavior had a statistically higher likelihood to report the following childhood experiences: hunting and fishing with parents as children, berry picking and mushroom collecting with parents as children, horseback riding, access to play in natural areas, and reading books about nature.

As was the case with the Wells and Lekies study, wild nature play, both unstructured and structured by parents but with the element of unpredictability in hunting and fishing and riding, were the experiences that seemed to incline the individual toward adult stewardship. In other words, it looks like activities that involve taking and eating (as opposed to just looking and learning), in conjunction with parents who model thoughtful use, are precursors to responsible environmental behavior.

"FOR SPECIAL PLACES to work their magic on kids," wrote lepidopterist Robert Michael Pyle, "they need to be able to do some clamber and damage. They need to be free to climb trees, muck about, catch things, and get wet—above all, to leave the trail." Luckily, there are numerous environmental education programs that allow children to play deeply in nature.

One organization that supports children's freedom to roam, play, even build on preserved land is the Harris Center for Conservation Education. The Harris Center is a New Hampshire education center and land trust with one of the most comprehensive family engagement and education programs in northern New England. The staff recognizes that many adults with environmental values speak fondly of childhood experiences like fort-building and attribute their land preservation values to these early experiences. Thus, one of their popular offerings for children is "The Forts, Shelters and Shanties Club." The public announcement reads, "Build it, live it and love it! If you love building forts and want to find out how to build different styles of forts, shelters and even shanties, here's your chance. Adventure awaits you in this club, as you create and build a wide range of different styles of outdoor and even a few indoor forts. Also included will be knot tying, fire building and wild tool construction."

During one afternoon a week for six weeks, children develop those foundational skills that were at the heart of Baden Powell's original conception of Scouting—woodcraft, living off the land, observation. And, from the Harris Center's perspective, they are also, hopefully, becoming future contributors to land preservation initiatives.

Wildly, gladly rejoicing together has taken root in the heartland as well. For a number of years, the Minnetrista gardens and cultural center in Muncie, Indiana, has conducted a Flower Fairies program. For three weeks prior to Midsummer's Eve, a dancer trains local children to each develop a flower fairy persona. This program started out being for girls, but when boys expressed an interest, they were allowed to participate as well. Each child chooses a flower, learns its attributes, and then develops a movement repertoire based on the flower's attributes. The child and teacher also develop a costume based on the appearance of the flower. For two or three nights around the summer solstice, the center invites the community to come stroll the brick pathways through the preserved Ball Estate Victorian gardens. The candlelit pathways are haunted with glimpses of flower fairies frolicking amid the azaleas, lilies, and periwinkles. A child's intrigue with fairies and the desire to be a fairy are used as the bridge to understanding the unique appearance and character of different flowers. Isn't this a foundational understanding of biodiversity? Wouldn't you rather do this than sit through Terri's PowerPoint?

For a particularly inspiring look at how things could be different, allow me to take you on a down-and-dirty outing with the Wilderness Youth Project in Santa Barbara, California. We assemble at Tucker's Grove County Park, a sliver of creek and forest nestled in between subdivisions.

Not really wilderness, but it feels wild enough and far enough away for children to feel immersed. There are about a dozen children aged seven to eleven—black, white, Latino—three leaders, and a handful of parents. The vibe is upbeat and energetic. No PowerPoints here. We circle up in the meadow and get our marching orders: explore our way up the dry streambed till we get to a sheltered pool with great mud for a mud fight.

Not far up the trail, there's a steep bank down to the dry creekbed. A couple of youngsters start to seat-slide down the crumbly bank. It's messy and a bit fast, yet there are no admonitions to stay on the trail. Rather, one leader goes down to the bottom to catch kids and dust them off, while another stays at the top to manage the flow. A few hundred yards up the trail, we come upon a fallen oak. Kids immediately jump up to balance beam, walk along the trunk and limbs, then jump off. It's a little risky. But instead of hustling them along, the leaders realize this kind of spontaneous play is exactly what the children need to be doing.

Round the next bend, we come to a fence with a gate. Most everyone goes through the gate, but one of the boys wants to try to climb over the fence, which is topped with a strand of barbed wire. I brace myself for the typical adult response, "No, José, you might rip your pants," or "Why don't you just go through the gate?" or "Let me lift you over," or "Please stop that! It's too dangerous." Instead, as soon as Kelly, one of the mentors, recognizes his intention, she says, "Great idea to try to climb over, José. Would you like me to spot you?" Once he's over, she crows, "Good job! I knew you could do it." I'm impressed that his intention is noticed, validated, and encouraged. Moreover, she refrains from overinvolvement, providing just enough support to make the process reasonably safe but letting him solve the problem. A supportive, can-do attitude prevails and fear is banished.

When we come upon a child-size fort made by a previous group to simulate a wood rat's nest, the children immediately start to crawl through it. Becka says, "This is so awesome. I am so not afraid in here. I could live here and do all my projects here." As soon as she is out, she says, "I'm going to do it again," and there was time for that.

A few minutes later some of the boys find a little hole in the trail and wonder what made it. They probe it with sticks and then decide to hide some treasures in it, cover it up, and look for it on the way back. An hour later—though it's hard to differentiate this stretch of trail from sections that look just like it, and no adult reminds them to look—they remember the spot and are thrilled to unearth an acorn, a marble rock, a sprig of clover. What an appropriate way to develop observation skills—all self-constructed by the children.

One of the kids captures a big, hoppy bug in his hands and shows it to Mark, one of the mentors. I prepare myself for the boring mini natural history lecture, "Oh, that's *Idiostatus aequalis*. We call it a California katydid and it lives only in the west-facing coastal chaparral slopes. It has six legs and three body parts—the head, abdomen, and the thorax, and blah, blah, blah ..." Instead, Mark says, "Hmm, I wonder what that is? Hey, how many legs does it have? Wow, look at those big eyes—they look kind of greenish to me. What color do they look like to you? What should we call this bug?" Later on, during a snack break, Mark pulls out an insect guide, finds the right page, and passes it to the children who had been looking at the insect. Instead of saying, "I think it's the California katydid," he says, "Does that bug we found on the trail look like any one of the bugs on this page?" The whole orientation is to encourage the kids to observe, wonder, see patterns, and make sense of things. Names and concepts, environmental knowledge emerged organically out of these hands-on explorations.

We arrive back at the meadow, wet, mud-smeared, laughing. One of the children says, unprompted, "Three hours isn't enough for these trips. We should do five hours. We should do all day! We should build forts and live out here." It was as if the children had dropped into their wild selves and become creatures of the woods, comfortable and at home in their minds, bodies, and native habitats. It had been just about a mile up and back, but so much had happened. There was never any talk about global warming or endangered species, but there was ample opportunity to become one with the natural world. And all the children were eager to come back and do it again.

This is the kind of environmental education that I believe leads to environmental values and behaviors in adulthood—education that originates in children's innate play tendencies in the natural world; supports and allows wild nature play; recognizes the importance of hunting, gathering, collecting, and, when appropriate, consuming the natural world; encourages adults and children to explore and learn together so adults can model attention and respect; and supports children's appetite for imagination and fantasy. It's environmental education that allows boys to live in Boyville, girls to live in Girlville, and kids to live in Kidville for a while before rushing them out of the woods into Adultville.

As John Burroughs once said, "Knowledge without love will not stick. But if love comes first, knowledge is sure to follow." It's our responsibility as parents and teachers to make sure that love comes first.

Medicine Grizzlybear Lake

AN INDIAN FATHER'S PLEA

DEAR TEACHER, I would like to introduce you to my son, Wind-Wolf. He was born and raised on the Reservation. He has black hair, dark brown eyes, and an olive complexion. And like so many Indian children his age, he is shy and quiet in the classroom. He is five years old, in kindergarten, and I cannot understand why you have already labeled him a "slow learner."

At the age of five, he has already had quite an education compared with his peers in Western society. As his first introduction into this world, he was bonded to his mother and to the Mother Earth in a traditional, native childbirth ceremony. And he has been continuously cared for by his mother, father, sisters, cousins, aunts, uncles, grandparents, and extended tribal family since this ceremony.

From his mother's loving arms, Wind-Wolf was placed in a secure and specially designed Indian baby basket. His father and the medicine elders conducted another ceremony to bond him with the essence of his genetic father, the Great Spirit, the Grandfather Sun, and the Grandmother Moon. This was all done in order to introduce him into the natural world and to protect his soul. It is our people's way of showing the newborn respect, ensuring that he starts life on the path of spirituality.

The traditional Indian baby basket became his "turtle's shell" and served as the first seat for his classroom. He was strapped in for safety, protected from injury by the willow roots and hazelwood construction. The basket was made by a tribal elder who had gathered her materials with prayer. It is specially designed to provide the child with the knowledge and experience he will need in order to survive in his culture and environment.

Wind-Wolf was strapped in snuggly with a deliberate restriction upon his arms and legs. Although you in Western society may argue that such a method serves to hinder motor-skill development and abstract reasoning, we believe it forces the child to first develop his intuitive faculties, rational intellect, symbolic thinking, and five senses. Wind-Wolf was with his mother constantly, closely bonded, as she carried him on her back or held him in front while breastfeeding. She carried him everywhere she went, and every night he slept with both parents. Because of this, Wind-Wolf's educational setting was not only "secure" but also colorful, complicated, and diverse. He has been with his mother at the ocean at daybreak when she made her prayers and gathered fresh seaweed from the rocks, he has sat with his uncles in a rowboat on the river while they fished with gill nets, and he has watched and listened to elders as they told creation stories and animal legends and sang songs around the campfires.

He has attended the sacred White Deerskin Dance of his people and is well acquainted with the cultures and languages of other tribes. He has been with his mother when she gathered herbs for healing and watched his tribal aunts and grandmothers gather and prepare traditional foods such as acorn, smoked salmon, and deer meat. He has played with abalone shells, pine nuts, iris grass string, and leather while watching the women make traditional regalia. He has had many opportunities to watch his father, uncles, and ceremonial leaders use different kinds of colorful feathers and sing different kinds of songs while preparing for the sacred dances and rituals.

As he grew older, Wind-Wolf began to crawl out of the baby basket and explore the world around him. When frightened or sleepy, he could always return to the basket, as a turtle withdraws into its shell. Such an inward journey allows one to reflect in privacy on what he has learned and to carry the new knowledge deeply into the unconscious and the soul. Shapes, sizes, colors, texture, sound, smell, feeling, taste, and the learning process are therefore integrated—the physical and spiritual, matter and energy, conscious and unconscious, individual and social.

Wind-Wolf was with his mother in South Dakota while she danced for seven days straight in the hot sun, in the sacred Sun Dance Ceremony of a distant tribe. He has been doctored in a number of different healing ceremonies by medicine men and women from places ranging from Alaska and Arizona to New York and California. He has been in more than twenty different sacred sweat lodge rituals—used by native tribes to purify mind, body, and soul—since he was three years old, and he has been exposed to many different religions of his racial brothers: Protestant, Catholic, Asian Buddhist, and Tibetan Lamaist.

It takes a long time to absorb and reflect on these kinds of experiences, so maybe that is why you think my Indian child is a slow learner. His aunts and grandmothers taught him to count while they sorted out the materials used to make the abstract designs in native baskets. He learned his basic numbers by helping his father count and sort the rocks to be used in the sweat lodge—seven rocks for a medicine sweat, say, or thirteen for the summer solstice ceremony. And he was taught mathematics by counting the sticks we use in our traditional native hand game. So I realize he may be slow in grasping the methods that you are now using in your classroom, but I hope you will be patient with him. It takes time to adjust to a new cultural system.

He is not culturally "disadvantaged," he is culturally "different." If you ask him how many months there are in a year, he will probably tell you thirteen. He will respond this way not because he doesn't know how to count properly, but because he has been taught by our traditional people that there are thirteen full moons in a year according to the native tribal calendar and thirteen tail feathers on a perfectly balanced eagle.

But he also knows that some eagles may have only twelve tail feathers, or seven. He knows that the flicker has exactly ten tail feathers, that they are red and black, representing east and west, life and death, and that this bird is a "fire" bird, a power used in native healing. He can count more than forty different kinds of birds, tell you what kind of bird each is and where it lives, the season in which it appears, and how it is used in a sacred ceremony. He may have trouble writing his name on a piece of paper, but he knows how to say it and many other things in several different Indian languages. He is not fluent yet because he is only five years old and required by law to attend your educational system, learn your language, your values, your ways of thinking, and your methods of teaching.

So you see, all of these influences together make him somewhat shy and quiet—and perhaps "slow" according to your standards. But if Wind-Wolf was not prepared for his first tentative foray into your world, neither were you appreciative of his culture. On the first day of class, you had difficulty with his name. You wanted to call him "Wind"—insisting that Wolf somehow must be his middle name. The students in the class laughed at him, causing him embarrassment.

While you are trying to teach him your new methods, he may be looking out the window as if daydreaming. Why? Because he has been taught to watch and study the changes in nature. It is hard for him to switch from the right to the left hemisphere of the brain when he sees the leaves turning bright colors, the geese heading south, and the squirrels scurrying to get ready for winter. In his heart, in his young mind, and almost by instinct, he knows that this is the time of year he is supposed to be with his people, gathering and preparing fish, deer meat, and plants and herbs, and learning his tasks in this role. He is caught between two worlds.

Yesterday, for the third time in two weeks, he came home crying and said he wanted to have his hair cut. He said he doesn't have any friends at school because they make fun of his long hair. I tried to explain to him that in our culture, long hair is a sign of masculinity and balance and is a source of power. But he remained adamant in his position.

To make matters worse, he recently encountered his first harsh case of racism. Wind-Wolf had managed to adopt at least one good school friend. On the way home from school one day, he asked his new pal if he wanted to come home to play with him until supper. That was okay with Wind-Wolf's mother, who was walking with them. When they got to the friend's house, the two boys ran inside to ask permission while Wind-Wolf's mother waited. But the other boy's mother lashed out, "It is okay if you have to play with him at school, but we don't allow that kind of people in our house!" When my wife asked why not, the other boy's mother answered, "Because you are Indians and we are white, and I don't want my kids growing up with your kind of people."

So now my young Indian child does not want to go to school anymore (even though his hair is cut). He feels that he does not belong. He is the only Indian child in your class, and instead of being proud of his race, heritage, and culture, he now feels ashamed. When he watches television, he asks why white people hate us so much and always kill our people in the movies and why they take everything from us. He asks why the other kids in school are not taught about the power, beauty, and essence of nature. Now he refuses to sing his native songs, play with his Indian artifacts, learn his language, and participate in his sacred ceremonies. When I ask him to go to an urban pow-wow or help me with a sacred sweat lodge ritual, he says no because "that's weird."

So, dear teacher, I want to introduce you to my son, Wind-Wolf. He stems from a long line of hereditary chiefs, medicine men and women, and ceremonial leaders whose knowledge is still studied and recorded in contemporary books. He has seven different tribal systems flowing through his blood; he is even part white. I want my child to succeed in school and in life. I don't want him to be a dropout or to end up on drugs and alcohol because he is made to feel inferior or because of discrimination. I want him to be proud of his rich culture, and I would like him to succeed in both cultures. But I need your help.

What you say and what you do in the classroom has a significant effect on my child. All I ask is that you work with me to help educate my child in the best way. If you don't have the knowledge and experience to deal with culturally different children, I am willing to help you with the few resources I have or direct you to other resources.

Millions of dollars have been appropriated by Congress each year for "Indian Education." All you have to do is encourage your school to use these resources. My Indian child has a constitutional right to learn and maintain his culture. By the same token I believe that non-Indian children have a constitutional right to learn about Native American heritage and culture, because Indians play a significant part in the history of Western society.

My son, Wind-Wolf, is not an empty glass coming into your class to be filled. He is a full basket coming into a different society with something special to share. Please let him share his knowledge, heritage, and culture with you and his peers.

Scott Russell Sanders

TOKENS OF MYSTERY

THERE IS A SAYING that you can take the boy out of the country but you cannot take the country out of the boy. My mother, who grew up in the steel-and-concrete hive of Chicago, frequently applied this remark with a roll of her eyes to my father, who grew up on a red dirt farm in Mississippi. It was true enough in this case, and it holds true for many another country boy and girl I have known, myself included. The legacy of a rural childhood entails more than a penchant for going barefoot, say, or an itch for digging in dirt, or a taste for black-eyed peas, or a habit of speaking with a lazy tongue. It also entails a relationship with the land, its rhythms and creatures. The country lingered in my father and lingers in me as a recollected intimacy with particular wild places, a memory of encounters with muskrats and mules, tornadoes and hickory trees, crickets and flooded creeks, the whole adding up to an impression of nature as grander, more intricate, and wiser in lots more ways than we two-leggers.

It is quite possible to grow up in the country without learning to honor nature. Drive the back roads of America, and you will see many a butchered forest, eroded field, and poisoned creek, many a trash dump, many a tattered animal shot up for the sheer joy of killing, all the handiwork of country people. In fact, the history of rural America has been largely one of slash and plunder. Familiarity with a landscape may breed no more than contempt if our eyes have been trained to see contemptuously, or it may breed devotion if we have learned to see reverently. In the book of Job, the beleaguered man cries out that all creatures, himself included, rest in the hand of God:

> But ask the beasts, and they will teach you;
> the birds of the air, and they will tell you;
> or the plants of the earth, and they will teach you;
> and the fish of the sea will declare to you.

The key word here is *ask*. What the birds and beasts and countryside teach us depends on the questions we pose. A person wielding a fifty-ton digger in search of coal will learn quite different lessons from one who wields a pair of binoculars in search of warblers. Job assumed that anybody who listened to the creation would hear the whisper of the Creator. But generally we hear what our ears have been prepared for, and if we do not go seeking divinity we are not likely to see or hear it. In the long run and in a blunt manner, nature has its own say; species that poison or exhaust their habitat die out. But in the short run, nature does not declare how we should approach it. That lesson we learn from culture.

For me as a child, "culture" meant first of all my parents, and then a few neighbors, then books and teachers, and only much later, when I was largely set in my ways, photographs and paintings and films. Whether plucking a pheasant, sawing down a tree, walking through the woods, planting beans, gathering blackberries, watching the moon, my parents acted out of a joyous, wondering regard for nature. To my mother, the budding of pussy willows or the reddening of maples announced the eras of our lives with more authority than anything the calendar or newspaper had to say. To my father, the paw prints of a raccoon in the mud beside a creek, or the persistent flowing of the creek itself, were tokens of an inexhaustible mystery. I learned from my parents a thousand natural facts, but above all I learned how to stand on the earth, how to address the creation, and how to listen.

Because of their example, I was drawn to those of our neighbors who shared this regard for nature—the elderly Swedish couple who let me help with maple sugaring, the carpenter who brooded on the grain in wood, the biology teacher who lived in a wild meadow (the sight of her musing among the waist-high flowers left a deeper impression on me than any lecture or textbook), the dairy farmers, horse trainers, muskrat trappers, hunters of fossils, feeders of birds. Their examples in turn prepared me to read with gusto about Mark Twain's Mississippi River, Thoreau's Walden Pond, Black Elk's High Plains, Anne Dillard's Roanoke Valley, Wendell Berry's Kentucky, Barry Lopez's Arctic, and the many other intimate landscapes in our literature.

I moved easily from literary visions of nature to visions inspired by science in the pages of Rachel Carson, Loren Eiseley, Lewis Thomas, and Stephen Jay Gould. Reading prepared me to relish the paintings of Thomas Cole and George Inness, the films of Jacques Cousteau, and music and ceremonies of Native Americans.

Thus begun on a path of ardent inquiry about the cosmos, I hope to make new discoveries so long as I live. Needless to say, I have not always lived up to these models for how one should dwell in nature—I close myself inside my human shell, I stop my ears and blinker my eyes, I squander the fruits of the earth—and yet, inscribed with those models of childhood, I always know when I have fallen away.

Meanwhile, just down the road from us lived a man and woman who whipped their horses, kicked their dogs, ruined their soil, and threw trash out the back door. Their children grew up doing likewise. Surrounded by the same landscape, the same beasts and weather as our family, these neighbors inhabited a radically different "nature" from the one we knew. Their conversation with the earth was carried on in a language foreign to the one I learned in my own household. You can grow up in the country and remain blissfully ignorant of nature, and you can behave as callously toward the earth as any city slicker. But still, love the land or hate it, attune yourself to its rhythms or mine it for dollars, the one thing you cannot do, having grown up in the country, is ignore it. You know in your bones that nature surrounds and sustains our tiny human play.

I AM NEVER MORE AWARE of being an overgrown backwoods boy than when I sojourn in a city. Transplanted this year from a small Indiana town, where deer still occasionally graze in backyards, to Boston, where the yards have been paved and deer pose on billboards, I find myself wondering how children in cities experience nature. When these children grow up, and some of them become the potentates who decide how we should protect the planet, what images of nature will govern their decisions? For me this is a question of private as well as public consequence because my 9-year-old son and 14-year-old daughter are sharing Boston with me. Having them on hand means I can snoop on youth without going far afield. I have emerged from some months of this snooping with a gloomy opinion of cities as places for learning about nature, but with an increased respect for the imagination, resourcefulness, and curiosity of children.

Suppose you are a child taking a walk in downtown Boston. What ghosts of wildness do you see amid the skyscrapers, glassy shops, condominiums, and parking lots? Well, you see dogs on leashes, sickly trees and shrubs (not quite on leashes, but planted in boxes and surrounded by fences to protect them from human assault), an occasional strip of grass that is kept alive by infusions of chemicals, cut flowers for sale on street corners, pigeons roosting on window sills, rats nosing in alleys. If you make your way to that fabled green space, the Public Garden, which is entirely hemmed in by a palisade of buildings, you will discover a concrete pond aswim with pinioned ducks (except after frost, when authorities drain the pool to avoid lawsuits), a row of elms bearing name tags, a cemetery, a baseball diamond, two subway stops, a six-lane boulevard, an expanse of trampled lawn planted with statues, and signs everywhere announcing what is forbidden. Since the avenues yield no glimpses of robust or unfettered nature, you might seek out water. But like most rivers that have the ill fortune to wind through cities, the Charles is a docile and filthy gutter, girded by walls, laced with bridges, hemmed in by highways, and slick with oil. The river's poisons collect in the harbor, which has become a gray desert encircled by shipyards, airport, docks, and high-rise apartments.

In this great outdoors of Boston, the only remnants of nature, aside from rats that look as though they might survive without our ministrations, are the sun and sky glimpsed overhead between glass towers. If you are bold enough to walk abroad at night, you will search for the stars in vain through the glare of streetlights. The breeze is laden with diesel fumes and the rumble of engines. By going indoors—into a shopper's nirvana such as Copley Place, for example, or a corporate stronghold such as the Prudential building—you can escape even the sky and its weathers, withdraw from seasons and the vagaries of sunlight.

In grocery stores, cows show up sliced and weighed into red hunks, chickens go featherless in styrofoam tubs, wheat disappears along with a dose of additives into gaudy packages, even apples and oranges wear a camouflage of dye. Day and night, indoors or out, nature in the city appears as a slavish power, rather puny and contemptible, supplying us with decoration, amusement, and food, always framed by our purposes, summoned or banished according to our whims.

Of course, like all reasonably affluent cities that take the burdens of enlightenment seriously, Boston provides its children with places to confront nature, as it were, in the flesh. Chief among these are the zoo, where morose animals pace in cages; the aquarium, where fish circle in tanks; the arboretum, where trees that never rub limbs in the wild grow side by side and bear identifying labels; and the science museum, where the university comes packaged in mind-sized dollops, usually jazzed up with electronics.

Fitted with a pair of child's eyes, let us pay a visit to the New England Aquarium. Outside you watch three seals cruise in a small, white, rhomboid-shaped pool. Two beats of the rear flippers carry them from end to end. You admire their grace, but soon realize that you have seen every move they are likely to make in such a cramped, sterile space. Inside the building, on the ground floor, you hang over the railing of a larger pool to observe a colony of jackass penguins, some of them zipping through the green shallows, some teetering across the fiberglass islands. Just when you are beginning to feel a sense of how these dapper birds might carry on in their natural realm, a diver splashes into the pool. From plastic buckets he doles out fish to the assembled penguins, noting on a clipboard the dietary selection for each bird. Meanwhile, from the balcony overhead, a second diver lowers a thermometer on a wire above the head of each pigeon in turn and records the temperatures on yet another clipboard. If you are like my son, you are distracted by the other kids who shoulder you aside for a view of the proceedings.

From the ground floor you climb a spiral ramp, passing tank after tank in which sea creatures browse or snooze in tiny simulated habitats— inky mud for the ocean depths, crashing surf for the coastal shallows, weedy thickets, and algal pools. These exhibits go some way toward showing us nature on its own terms, as a web of life, a domain of nonhuman forces. And yet these miniature habitats with their listless swimmers are still merely pictures framed and labeled by their masters; they are images viewed, like those on television, through windows of glass.

From the top floor you gaze down into a huge, cylindrical tank, which houses a four-story fiberglass replica of a coral reef and several hundred species of fish. The size of it, the painted reefs, the mixture of species all give some feel for the larger patterns of the sea. And yet immediately a naturalist begins lecturing while a diver descends to feed the sharks. "You think they'll bite him?" the children ask, their minds bearing Hollywood images of underwater killers, nature measured on a scale of menace. By means of another ramp you spiral down along the circumference of this tank, stopping to press your nose through a watery thickness of glass against the snout of a moray eel. This is communion of a sort. Downstairs, a film about the artificial reef celebrates the imitation more than the ocean's original, dwelling on the ingenuity of the builders, the strength of the walls, the weight of glass and steel, thereby confirming your sense that nature is fortunate indeed to have been packaged by such clever artisans.

A bell rings, calling you to the 11 o'clock water show. You rush to the auditorium, squeeze into a seat, then watch as the trainer puts a seal and three dolphins through their paces. An earnest woman, the trainer carries on about how intelligent these animals are, how cantankerous, how creative, but all you see are dolphins jumping through hoops and retrieving rubber toys, a seal balancing a ball on its nose and smacking its flippers at jokes; all you hear are the synchronized splashes, whistles, and grunts of programmed clowns.

Visit the zoo in Franklin Park—or any zoo, even the most spacious and ecologically minded—and you will find nature parceled out in showy fragments, a nature demeaned and dominated by our constructions. Thickets of bamboo and simulated watering holes cannot disguise the elementary fact that a zoo is a prison. The animals are captives, hauled to this place for our edification or entertainment. No matter how ferocious they may look, they are wholly dependent on our care. A bear squatting on its haunches, a tiger lounging with half-lidded eyes, a bald eagle hunched on a limb like refugees who tell us less about their homeland, their native way of being, than about our power. In the zoo they exist without purposes of their own, cut off from their true place on earth and from the cycles demanded by their flesh.

Visit the Museum of Science, a lively playhouse aimed at luring children into a reasoned study of the cosmos, and again you find nature whittled down to fragments. Most of the exhibits have to do, not with nature, but with our inventions—satellites, steam engines, airplanes, computers, telephones, lasers, robots, cars, Van de Graaf generators—a display of human power that merely echoes the lessons of the city. As though to compensate, a number of creaturely exhibits are gigantic—a full-scale model of *Tyrannosaurus rex*, a grasshopper the size of a delivery van, an immense brain (ours, of course, thereby reminding us where the center of the cosmos lies). But no matter how large, the beasts themselves are manifestly artificial, further proof of our ingenuity. "Wow," cry the children. "How did they make *this*?" The nearest you can come to nature's own products is in the hall of dioramas, where stuffed animals, encased in glass, pose in habitat groups against painted backdrops. How long will you stand before these dusty, silent, rigid carcasses, while elsewhere in the museum, our own handiworks beckon with luminous colors, bright lights, synthetic voices, and flashy movements?

On the wall of the museum there is a quotation from Aristotle: "The search for Truth is in one way hard and in another easy—for it is evident that no one of us can ever master it fully, nor miss it wholly. Each one of us adds a little to our knowledge of nature, and from all the facts assembled arises a certain grandeur." Worthy sentiments; yet the facts assembled in the museum, like the bits of nature scattered through the city, point to no grandeur except our own. So long as we meet nature in fragments and in human containers, we cannot see it truly. Even when science is called in to explain what we are beholding, it comes not so much as a way of reading the cosmos, but as an instrument of power. Without wishing to deny the educational zeal of those who run the museum, the zoo, the aquarium, or the other city areas for the display of nature, I want to emphasize how belittling, how dangerously one-sided are the impressions these arenas create. Sight of stuffed antelope, trees behind fences, gorillas behind bars, penguins in tanks, and flowers in pots will more likely inspire contempt than awe. Snared in our inventions, wearing our labels, the plants and animals stand mute. In such places, the loudest voice we hear is our own.

NONE OF THE FOREGOING is meant as a diatribe against Boston in particular—a place I delight in—nor against cities in general, but rather as a sober account of the peculiar, even pathological image of nature the city provides. Recognizing how distorted this image is, we should feel the necessity of making available to our children a wiser and healthier one. Although my view of cities as places for learning about nature is gloomy, my view of children as learners is hopeful. Against all odds, many an urban child acquires a sense of the dignity, integrity, and majestic self-sufficiency of nature. How does this come about? For the beginnings of an answer, let me describe a recent conversation with my son, Jesse.

One day this past winter he and I set out for the library on foot. Whenever Jesse steps outdoors, all his senses come alert. Before we have even crossed the street, he has squatted down to examine a slab of ice in the gutter. The slab had broken in two, and the pieces, gliding on their own melt water, had slipped a hand's width apart. After a moment of scrutiny, tracing the ice with a finger, he observed, "These are like continents drifting apart on molten rock."

This led us to discuss the geological theory of plate tectonics, about which we had seen a documentary on television. According to the theory, earthquakes are caused by the friction of adjoining plates as they rub against one another. We tried this out on the ice, shoving the two pieces together until their edges grated, and were rewarded by the feel of tremors passing through our gloved hands. Continuing our walk to the library, we recalled what a friend of the family, a seismologist, had told us about his study of earthquakes in the Soviet Union and what that study had revealed about the structure of the earth.

"I read in school, " Jesse told me excitedly, "that Chinese scientists have discovered a kind of fish that can feel when earthquakes are coming, even before machines can."

In reply, I told how one time James Jacques Audubon was riding near the Ohio River, when his usually obedient horse stopped dead in its tracks and spread its legs as though to keep from tumbling over. 'What in blazes?' Audubon thought. Neither word nor whip could make the horse budge—and a good thing, too, for several minutes later the ground buckled and the trees rocked from the New Madrid earthquake.

"You know," Jesse mused, "lots of animals have keener senses than we do. Like the way coon dogs can smell, and the way birds can travel using landmarks and stars and earth's magnetism."

He had learned of coon dogs from one of his grandfather's stories, of celestial navigation from a visit to a whaling museum, of migration from magazines and from our habit of watching, every spring and fall, for the unerring movements of ducks and geese overhead. We then talked about the night vision of owls and the daylight vision of ospreys, birds we had seen on our camping trips.

"If I could see like an eagle," said Jesse, "I'd be able to spot tiny things like field mice from way high up. But would I be able to see in color?"

Since that question stumped me, and since by then we had reached the library, we decided to look up the answer. None of the books gave a clear-cut answer, but one of them did say that birds of prey owe their acute vision to the dense packing of rods and cones in their retinas. From the dictionary we then learned that rods are sensitive to dim light, cones to bright light and colors. So we had our answer, and in our excitement, we gave one another a boisterous high-five hand slap that provoked a glower from the librarian.

In skimming the encyclopedia articles, Jesse had noticed that birds have a rapid heartbeat. How fast was his own? How fast was his pulse? Eighty beats per minute. How fast was mine? Fifty-five. How come his was faster? I told him it was partly because of our relative size—small bodies lose heat more quickly than large ones—and partly because children have a higher rate of metabolism than adults. What's metabolism? Jesse wanted to know. So we talked about how cells turn food into energy and tissue.

"Like we get energy from milk," said Jesse, "and the cow gets energy from grass, and the grass gets energy from the sun. I bet if you go back far enough, you can track every kind of food to the sun."

By now, our rucksacks filled with a new supply of books, we were moseying toward home. On the way, Jesse kept up his flurry of questions and speculations. Could humans live by eating grass? Why doesn't grass use up the soil and wear it out? How much grass would a big wild critter like a buffalo have to eat every day to stay alive? Smoke rising from a chimney then set him talking about wind patterns, acid rain, forests. If bad chemicals fall on the grass—lead, say, from diesel trucks—and cattle graze on it, and we eat the cattle in our hamburgers, the poison winds up in us, right? And so, within the space of an hour, driven by Jesse's curiosity, we moved from a broken slab of ice to the geology of the earth, from earthquakes to eagles, from the anatomy of the eyes to the biology of food chains. Out front of our place one of Jesse's buddies led him off to play hockey.

Such conversations do not happen every day, but they happen frequently enough to persuade me that Jesse, at age nine, is persistently, eagerly building a model of nature, one that will make sense of the full variety of his experience. As that experience enlarges, so he continually revises his model. In this one conversation he drew from books, magazines, school, radio and television (public radio and public television; to seek knowledge of nature on the commercial channels is like searching for a moose in a parking lot), drew from his memories of camping trips, gardening, hikes in the woods, seaside rambles, mealtime conversations, family stories, visits to museums, talks with adult friends (a geologist, a physician, a bird-watcher, a farmer)—he drew from all these sources in an attempt to see nature whole. He needed every scrap of this experience, and would have used anything else his nine years might have provided.

Jesse shares with all children this voracious hunger to make sense of things, but his *way* of making bears the stamp of his upbringing. Having lived most of his nine years in a house with a wildflower garden in the backyard, in a small town surrounded by forests and creeks, having known farmers and stone quarries and biologists, and having spent many hours with his family tramping through the countryside, he knows without being told that nature is ultimately our home. What the city has to say about nature—in museums, zoos, parks—he understands in light of what he has already learned from the country. Watching California gray whales migrate along the Pacific coast prepared him to view without condescension the dolphins that jump through hoops. Because he has watched pileated woodpeckers graze on dead trees and white-tailed deer cross a meadow like ripples of pure energy, he knows that beasts in cages are lords in exile.

In Thoreau's exultant phrase, "We need to witness our own limits transgressed, and some life pasturing freely where we never wander." This is all the more crucial for urban children who live in a maze of human invention. If a child is to have an expansive and respectful vision of nature, there is no substitute for direct encounters with wildness. This means passing un-programmed days and weeks in the mountains, the woods, the fields, beside rivers and oceans, territories where plants and beasts are the natives and we are the visitors. Ideally children should witness "life pasturing freely" in the company of adults who are intimately aware of nature's pulse and pattern. As parents, we can assure our children of such company, not by turning them over to experts, but by cultivating this awareness in our selves.

My own parents never *told* me how I should feel about nature; they communicated their own deep regard for that larger order by their manner of living. On hearing the call of geese, my father would drop whatever he was doing and rush outside. On visiting a new place, he would scoop up a handful of dirt to get the feel of it, the smell and the taste of it. When I was small enough to ride in his arms, during thunderstorms he would bundle me in a blanket and carry me onto the porch and hold me against his chest while we listened to the rain sizzle down. My mother would tramp across a bog to admire a lady-slipper or a toad. When I first came across Dylan Thomas's fierce lines,

> The force that through the green fuse drives the flower
> Drives my green age; that blasts the roots of trees
> Is my destroyer.

it was a truth I had already learned from her. She was alive to designs everywhere—in the whorls of her palm and the spirals of a chambered nautilus, in the crystals of milky quartz, the flukes of a mushroom, the whiskers of a mouse. Neither of my parents was a scientist, but they were both eager to learn everything science could tell them about the workings of the world.

Fashioning a vision of nature is one of the urgent enterprises of childhood. I believe that Jesse's curiosity, his desire to understand and feel at home on the earth, is typical of young children. The child inhabits a compact wilderness called the body, with which he or she reaches out to all other living things. Look at a child and see an organism perfectly equipped for investigating the world: wide-awake eyes, quick brain, avid mouth, irrepressible hands. Nothing is lost on children, so long as it brings news from previously unknown regions. Their questions not only probe the universe; they probe us. How much do we understand of the workings of the cosmos and of our place within it? Where are we ignorant? Do we know how (or care) to search for answers? Daily companionship with a questioning child is a reminder of what intelligence is *for*—not for domination, but for communion.

Children are transcendentalists by instinct, reading in the humblest natural fact a sign of some greater pattern. Unlike a grown-up, who might often with more accuracy be called a grown-rigid, children will only settle for a cramped, belittling view of nature if that is what we offer them. So let us offer them tokens of the creation, that elegant wildness, that encompassing order which calls for our own powers of understanding and, when mind has stretched as far as it will go, for love.

Kelly McMasters

LESSONS OF A STARRY NIGHT

A Rachel Carson essay teaches a new mother how to imbue her growing child with an awe of nature.

A FEW MONTHS after my son was born in August 2009, I read Rachel Carson's essay "The Sense of Wonder." Written in 1956 and published in *Woman's Home Companion* magazine in July of that year, the essay offered suggestions for fostering connections between children and nature, something I had hoped to do with my son, and I looked forward to hearing more from a woman and writer I admired so much. Carson never had any children of her own, but in "The Sense of Wonder" she shares memories of time spent with her young nephew: a nighttime visit to the ocean, a rainy walk in the woods, listening to soft whispers of wind and insects. She designed the work to be a kind of instruction manual for parents, assuring them that even if they don't know the difference between a sandpiper and a plover, they could work to instill an appreciation for nature in their children. As with most of her writing, a discomfort lingers just beneath the surface, a warning. I hadn't expected a sunny children's story, but the darkness was unsettling.

According to Carson's essay, "A child's world is fresh and new and beautiful, full of wonder and excitement. It is our misfortune that for most of us that clear-eyed vision, that true instinct for what is beautiful and awe-inspiring, is dimmed and even lost before we reach adulthood." At the time I read these words, my family was splitting our life between Manhattan and rural northeastern Pennsylvania, and in the beginning years of making a home in the country. I'd felt the natural instinct and

73

awareness Carson talks about slowly return to me. Our small 1860s farmhouse is in the middle of hundreds of undeveloped acres full of soft hemlock forests and ferns, rambling rock walls and thorny rose bushes, nut-brown grouse and barn swallows. During the ten years I'd lived in the city full-time, my life was all dark angles, hard surfaces, sharp shadows. But after a few days in the country, it was as though my brain snapped open and color flooded in—the shock of the shimmering gold heads of the skinny poplars in the pasture out back, the soft, salmon newts with their purple, diamond-studded backs darting through the leaves, the electric lime of the new grass under the last of the melting snow—all arriving in a magnificent sensory rush.

The winter I was pregnant, I marched in the fresh snow around our front field in my boots and heavy coat while my husband puttered in the barn, the large sliding door cinched open, the first floorboards dusted white. I was just big enough for my stomach to get in the way of things, grazing the steering wheel or the edge of the washing machine as I bent to pull out a load of clothes. I missed my body, or rather, I missed being certain of my body, of where it began and ended. It no longer moved as quickly as I commanded. I tromped around, feeling fidgety, and flung myself onto my back in the snow.

I felt the cold on my neck and thighs and watched the gray sky, clouds moving fast. From my spot in the front of the barn I stared into the branches of a cherry tree arching over me, the frozen buds enclosed in ice. I shut my eyes and let the hard, metallic smell of the snow into my lungs. When the wind blew, a sound like pencils snapping echoed through the air, the tree cracking its thin frozen shell.

After a while, I could hear my husband tamping ice, then smelled the sawdust as he spread handfuls of the curled, yellow shavings out near my car so I wouldn't slip. I placed my hand on my stomach and imagined I could feel that heat of my belly through my think coat, a small furnace working hard. I thought of things I hadn't thought of for a very long time, like igloos and hot chocolate, mittens linked together with string, the magic of snowflakes and icicles. For so long, winter had just been something to shovel out or drive through. Sinking down into the hillside, I remembered how, as a child, those hours playing in the snow felt unwavering and enchanted, as if winter would last forever, time suspended and caught in a snow globe. I looked forward to returning to this time through my own child's eyes.

In her essay Carson suggests, "Exploring nature with your child is largely a matter of becoming receptive to what lies all around you. It is learning to use your eyes, ears, nostrils and fingertips, opening up the disused channels of sensory impression." Pregnancy is a good exercise for this state of hyperawareness. When a craving was satisfied—the tart squirt of a wedge of grapefruit or a mouthful of bitter arugula—I felt as if I'd doused a fire. I could smell everything: a student's coffee from across the classroom, the spit of beer left in the bottom of a can in the recycling bucket, the first flowering of milkweed on the hill. I felt as though I had both my son's and my own senses coursing through my body.

The morning of his birth, I sat in the bathtub and traced the knob of his elbow beneath my stretched skin. Understanding that today would be the last day I'd get to see that elbow, I began to mourn his absence within me. Never again would we be so close, so safe. And yet, even after our cord was cut, we'd remain tethered. What Carson felt between her own fingertips and nature, the opening of that disused channel of sensory impression, was the same. A connectedness that exists whether we want it to or not, even if we've lost our ability to see it.

WHEN MY SON WAS five months old, my car hit a patch of ice not far from our house. It was early January and the first day that snow wasn't falling after a long stretch of storms. The sun was bright and the sky blue, but as I rounded a corner between a pasture and bog, I came upon a section of road where snow has just drifted over, hiding a slick scrim of ice on the blacktop. I felt the tires go out first, a horse losing her hind legs. I turned the steering wheel, thought I'd come out of it. But then the car spun and I was backwards until the driver's side hit the bank of snow on the edge of the road and I felt the car go over. I thought to myself, "So *this* is happening." I gripped the steering wheel hard and closed my eyes as the car rolled and rolled and rolled.

The first thing I heard was silence. The first thing I smelled was the woods. I opened my eyes and slowly understood that I was hanging upside down by the strap of my seatbelt. My arms were still locked straight out in front of me, hands still gripping the steering wheel. The sharp trunk of an evergreen had broken through and nearly impaled the passenger seat next to me. The loamy smell of the sap was thick in the air, and I heard the crack of thin ice breaking, the sound of a winter walk through the woods, boots crunching through the frozen mud of a trail. I looked above (below?) my head and saw the moon roof, still shattering, spidery breaks crisscrossing the glass, opening to the darkness of the ground.

When I finally released my belt and crawled out on the back of the car, pushing aside my son's empty carseat dangling limply upside down, I stumbled out into the snow. Minutes had passed—maybe five? fifteen?— and no one had arrived. No other cars were on the road when I careened off and no other cars had gone by since. I took a few steps through the deep snow, my legs heavy, my head cloudy and off-balance, and fell into a drift. I stayed there for a moment and went through a checklist: legs? arms? I seemed fuzzy, but fine. My glasses were still on my nose—not even a scratch. The top of my head ached where I'd smashed into the metal roof again and again as I rolled, my body bouncing up and down like a pogo stick, but when I reached up, I was surprised to feel no blood there, only the soft tassel of my hat. The wind blew over me, and I watched the top of a nearby pine push slowly to the side. The silence, the smell of the pines and the snow, the deep, dark green against the bright white—everything seemed amplified, preternatural.

I reflexively placed my hands on my stomach, but the flatness there was as quiet as the wind through the pasture. My son was home, a few miles away. I'd left his father with a kit to make a mold of the baby's feet and hands, a craft project while I spent the afternoon with a local library reading group. This was the first time I had taken the car without my son, one of the first times I'd even driven since his birth.

Later, at the hospital, I lay on a bed for hours until the MRI machine was free. My husband and son were in the waiting room. My mind swimming, breasts swelling with milk, I wondered how much time had passed and worried about the baby who must be hungry, just a few hundred feet away. But my husband had thought quickly, swiping a bottle and packs of emergency breast milk from the freezer, stuffing them into the baby bag along with an extra outfit and diapers. They were fine in the waiting room without me.

I COULDN'T DRIVE for the rest of the winter. We passed the scene of the accident whenever we went to town; over time, the cracked tree sank into the snow, its needles turning from green to brown and finally falling from the limbs until the pine resembled some broken carcass, a pile of bones on the side of the road.

We continued to go back and forth between the city and our home in the country. I found myself staring out at the stretch of white, the frozen landscape reflecting my own fear while I waited for the thaw. I found comfort in Carson's words: "There is something so infinitely healing in the repeated refrains of nature—the assurance that dawn comes from night, and spring after the winter." But only when early morning birdsong returned to the dark woods did I truly believe spring would come again.

By April the snow finally melted in Pennsylvania. We started returning to the country more often, and I assumed I'd start driving soon. I planned to bury my car keys—the only part left of the totaled, black Subaru—next to the skeleton of the fallen tree once the ground thawed. Then one day the tree disappeared. All that remained was a crooked stump. I tried to drive, but just wound up sitting in our pickup truck in the dirt driveway, saying, *After the next song I'll go, after the NEXT song.* In July, I noticed from the passenger seat that some daisies had pushed up alongside the stump, a small ring of white. The scar on the ground left by the car was nearly healed. The wooden marker, the simple flowers, the mounded earth all reminded me of what I'd narrowly escaped. My breath caught in my throat each time my family and I drove by.

Returning to the farmhouse one night, having tried not to look at the broken space in the pines as we passed the accident site, I lifted my son out of his carseat while my husband took our bags inside. I pulled his small body out into the deep darkness and let his head droop against my collarbone like a folded flower. He was not afraid of the night, but in the space between the darkened porch and the blue silhouette of the barn, I tried not to guess how many pairs of eyes stared at us from the forest or to think about the coyotes calling from the swamp. I forced myself not to calculate how many steps it would take to get to the front door, how much time I would need to fish out the keys from my pocket. I worked hard to not let him feel my fear.

I thought of Carson's essay instead and cupped the back of his head in my palms so we could both look up. The sight of the stars washed across my face like a splash of yellow from a flashlight. I listened to his breathing, felt his heartbeat through his back. We looked quietly into the night sky, the kind you get only when far from the manmade blaze of cities and towns, more stars than sky nearly, like a spray of flour on a cutting board. I whispered to him about the ghost swirl of the Milky Way, the blinking satellites, a planet glowing pink above the barn. My face close to his, I watched him watch the stars until he saw them, really saw them. Finally he lifted his small arm and pointed to the sky, turning his amazed face to mine, as if to say, "Have you seen this, Mama?"

Near the end of "The Sense of Wonder," Carson writes, "Those who contemplate the beauty of the earth find reserves of strength that will endure as long as life lasts." But whose life did she mean? In 1957, the year after she wrote the essay, Carson's young nephew Roger, who is the center of her story, became her charge when his mother died. And one year later after that her own mother, with whom Carson had lived for most of her adult life, also died. Cancer would take Carson herself in 1964. I imagine the two of them in Maine before this, though, motherless daughter and newly motherless son, standing on the rocks between her cottage and the ocean, breathing in the salt and sea, staring into the bright, night sky, speaking to each other the names of the shells and the birds dotting the shoreline, feeling less alone than we might assume.

IN THE FALL, I finally drove for the first time. Not far, but far enough. We started talking about staying in the country full-time, but for a while we continued to go back and forth. I realized that a year would come and go and then it would be winter and I'd just have to try to drive again in the spring. The three weeks preceding the crash, including my son's first Christmas, had been wiped out of my brain from the concussion I'd suffered when my skull cracked against the car roof, and I was slowly accepting that the memories would likely never return to me.

Instead, I used Carson's essay as a blueprint to create more memories, to help with the heartbreak that lingered when I thought about how nearly not just my memories disappeared because of that crash. I thought of my boys sitting in the hospital waiting room, wondered how long the cache of frozen breast milk would have lasted, what my son would have remembered about me, if anything at all. My family was safe now, I would remind myself, but I knew we would never really be as safe as on that faraway morning in the bathtub, my son's small body still curled inside me, my husband asleep upstairs.

And so I concentrated on building a trail of breadcrumbs, as Carson suggested, using the natural world to establish a channel of connection. My son was young, barely a year old, but I hoped somehow, if and when I was finally lost to him, he might be able to see my hands in the soft brown of the garden's soil, know that I would still be there in the strands of honey-wheat waving, in the feathery fingers of the hemlocks at his collar, and in the blaze of stars in the open, night sky I showed him when he was a baby.

In October, as my husband and I tucked small ear-shaped cloves of garlic into the ground, the season's first snowflakes began to fall. We celebrated, relieved to get the garlic covered just in time, and then turned to our son, who had been sitting contentedly at the edge of the rows, dwarfed by the tall fence circling the remnants of our summer vegetable garden. He was looking up, smiling, mouth open. The flakes were huge and movie-white, snow-globe snow. I squatted next to him and held out my hand, and his eyes followed one of the large flecks of snow as it landed on my dirt-covered palm and disappeared, melting into my skin. He stared at my hand, then looked into my face. Do it again, Mama. And we sat there, the two of us, snow swirling in the small circle space enclosed by our garden fence, my husband humming as he covered the mounds of dirt with leaves so the crows wouldn't tease out the garlic; our son staring at us both, working hard to understand, to remember; and me with my hand out, trying my best to hold onto the idea of wonder.

Pattiann Rogers

CRADLE

I CANNOT THINK OF anything more important for the future of the earth than that we have loving, diligent mothers and fathers caring for our children. Nothing. We can write books and make speeches and conduct research and discuss data and theories and hold seminars and establish educational programs and pass laws and levy fines and set aside wilderness areas and protect endangered species, but none of these will make much difference to the future well-being of the earth unless we have children entering adulthood who are confident enough of their own worth to be able to love generously, to give to others, to make sacrifices, to restrain their desire for possessions—adults who understand how honesty, loyalty, justice, and benevolence come into being only through personal action.

If children learn to act with compassion by being treated compassionately themselves, if they learn to love by being loved, to respect others by having received respect, to cooperate by being involved in cooperation, to keep their word by experiencing honesty, to protect others by having been protected themselves—how can we possibly overestimate the importance of children being nurtured by dependable parents who are capable of demonstrating such qualities? It will be these qualities that will form the bases for all future decisions our children must make regarding their interactions with other people and the natural world.

For these reasons, the reliable presence of the attentive mother in a child's life has always seemed crucial to me. No one loves a child with a forgiving and enduring love like his or her own mother. No one else is so intensely concerned with her child's welfare, no one else so fierce in the defense of her child, no one else so quick to allay fears, to reassure, no one else so attuned to her child's needs. In those early years of life when a child is unsure and awkward, lacking skill with language, attempting to negotiate in a world of often critical and commanding adults without fully understanding what is expected, there must be a shelter, a place of steady love and acceptance. That place of trust is most often the mother.

Before the births of my own children, when I was teaching school, I used to watch my kindergarten children waiting for their mothers to come for them at the end of the day. I always saw an intense joy and confidence on the face of each one as his or her mother came into sight: "This is my mother." That same joy was never quite there for any other adult.

The security and love given by a father is very important also, of course. I loved my own father dearly, and I remember the feeling I had as a young daughter when held in his arms. (A friend once told me that as a child in bed alone in the dark at night, he always felt the world was safe as long as he could hear his father's voice.) I'm certain my confidence in my father's love has contributed to my feelings of confidence in the existence of a protective, benevolent divinity, a cognizant and responsive universe in which I possess value and purpose. And, as a mother, I could explain things to my sons, but they needed their father at every stage of their growth in order to come to some understanding of what a man is. But for now my emphasis is on the role of the mother, and to paraphrase Adrienne Rich: Every child deserves a mother who thinks he, or she, is a miracle.

Being a mother is a hard job to do well. It's a job that demands time and concentration—it can't be hurried, it can't be scheduled. It requires intelligence, creativity, patience, and stamina. It involves emotional risk, an identification with the body and soul of another human being, a giving that is unique. The work of love is exquisitely painful, my friend, Jim Whitehead, said to me not long ago.

Almost any other employment or profession can seem to offer a brighter future, less emotional risk, more tangible rewards (a paycheck), respect given more often by the community. (I wouldn't want to count the times I've heard the question, "Do you work or are you a housewife?") No wonder so many women, despite bearing children, have largely abandoned the responsibilities of being mothers, to the detriment of the society and its ability to act with prudence and circumspection.

Many women, in circumstances beyond their control, must work outside the home, and children of these mothers need special attention from friends and relatives. If one of the reasons for marriage is to establish an environment for raising healthy children, then keeping the family unit intact will allow many mothers the option of being at home with their children, at least through those very early years when self-image and important attitudes toward life are being formed.

I was recently reminding my older son, who is grown now, of an incident in his childhood when he was around eight years old. My father had passed away that year. Before his death he'd given my son a BB pistol that shot a single BB, loaded one at a time. My son came rushing into the house one day after school, shouting that he was going to get his BB pistol and shoot Timmy Gilmore, an infamous neighborhood bully.

I followed him in his fury into his bedroom, attempting to find out how he'd been hurt, what had happened, trying to urge him to consider other courses of action, hoping not to be forced to embarrass him by restraining him physically.

"Grandpa would want me to do this," he shouted in anger, evidencing an impression of manhood—protecting the dignity of the family—that had somehow been conveyed to him. This stance hurt me in its pathos—a young boy attempting to live up to the conceived image of his grandfather who was gone.

Well, my son didn't shoot anybody with his BB pistol, that day or any other. I listened and sympathized with his outrage, until his temper cooled and we could talk a little more about his pistol and about people who do cruel things.

We were laughing about this affair, because my adult son, a thoughtful, levelheaded individual, is so different from this angry child bent on physical violence, when my younger son, who was reminiscing with us, said to me, "But what if you hadn't been there?"

Children need our attentive presence. Despite their many virtues, children are not born civilized, and I mean by that not born knowing how to negotiate the world with self-control, courtesy, and restraint. Most mothers, when they turn their full attention to their children, are so good at helping them acquire these qualities, so very good at being mothers. They can easily become experts at it—feeding, nursing, comforting and encouraging, dressing and bathing (not simply as chore, but as communication with careful hands that cherish and respect), listening, correcting and sympathizing, teaching the stories and songs, teaching the language, daily defining for the child what being human can and must mean.

There is a difference between maintaining children and nurturing children, the difference between feeding the body and feeding the soul. How do we best nurture children? I think we begin by all of us, the whole society, everyone, acknowledging the skill and love and time it takes to do the work properly, emphasizing again and again, and never forgetting, how important it is that the job be done well, both for the society of human beings and for the health of the natural world. We must recognize and encourage, with all moral and practical support possible, those who are engaged in the task.

I say without hesitation that nothing done on this earth is more important for the earth than what mothers and fathers together have the power and talent to do.

CHILDREN ARE HIGHLY INTELLIGENT, capable creatures who have a unique rapport with the natural world. I often prefer their company to the company of adults, simply for their wide-ranging curiosity, their ease and delight with the earth, their openness and flexibility.

Anyone who has been around children and paid attention to them is aware of these qualities. I remember noticing my 2-year-old son one cold autumn morning, hunkered down on the sidewalk looking closely at a small gathering of water. When I got down on the sidewalk and looked too, I saw tiny needles of frost, white and crystalline, perfectly aligned, circling the pool of water. Understanding his wonder at seeing such strange and intricate beauty for the first time, I was captivated myself: Why and what was this beauty, this joy in the beholding?

And I agreed with my 4-year-old son John, watching a small catfish he'd caught as it swam in its bucket of water, when he said to me in hushed and heartfelt tones, "It's the most beautiful thing I ever saw in my life."

"I brought my child into this world," I heard a young mother say. "The least I can do is let him show it to me."

Even adolescents can demonstrate an enlivening connection with the earth. Once when we were driving through the Front Range of the Rockies and had stopped at a scenic overlook, an old truck with three scraggly-looking teenage boys came roaring in beside us. All three jumped out in their raucous, careless way, leaving the doors wide open, music blaring. One boy, bounding to the top of a boulder, looked out over the enormous valley below, the overwhelming blue rock mass of Mt. Evans rising in the background, and shouted in truly awestruck tones, "Holy Freak Show!"

My rather calm contemplation of the scene was suddenly charged with new exuberance.

Most children have a relationship with the earth we can learn from, a relationship of curiosity and acceptance, free of barriers or judgments, a melding of the body with the natural world. Adults, by acknowledging the intelligence and perception of children, by allowing themselves, when circumstances arise, to be taught by children (not in a patronizing way but with genuine attention and interest) are teaching that learning and curiosity are ongoing activities, that questioning is an enjoyable pursuit, that it is not shameful to admit ignorance, that praise of all forms of life engenders strength. Listening carefully to children and considering what they have to say also gives them a measure of self-respect and enables them to obey adults more readily, without feeling constantly humiliated or demeaned.

One spring morning when we were living in Texas, I saw my son Artie, around two and a half at the time, follow our cat Moby into our garage. Dangling lifelessly from Moby's mouth was a small lizard, an anole, head hanging from the jaws on one side, thread of a tail swinging from the other.

Artie emerged from the garage a minute later carrying the anole, draped motionless as a limp ribbon over his finger. Rather than the normal vivid yellow-green, the anole was an ashen, purple-gray. His eyes were lidded and sunken away. His tiny feet and hair-thin toes were drooping and still.

"He's dead, Artie," I said.

"He *not* dead," Artie said, emphatically.

"The cat caught him and killed him, Artie. He's dead," I repeated, pointing out the still eyes, the small tear in the skin at the anole's neck, the way the anole was lying stomach-up now, inert, unresponsive, head tilted back, in Artie's palm.

"He *not* dead," Artie insisted. "He not dead." There was something of faith in his tone. So, to placate Artie, I got a paper cup, and we put the anole, who slid with no resistance at all, into the bottom of it. No need for a lid—he was dead. I put the cup on a window sill in the kitchen and went on doing other things and so did Artie.

A few minutes later, working at the kitchen sink, I glanced at the cup, and behold! it was empty. For a moment, I had a surge of astonishment and joy that must have been at least a little similar to Mary Magdalene's when she saw the empty tomb with the stone rolled away.

And there, rushing up the bright window pane, was the "dead" anole, his body full and alert, pulsing sun-green, his agile legs and toes spread, his head cocked, his black eyes, deep as day, staring right at me.

Resurrection.

I had been wrong, not realizing how superbly anoles can "play dead" as a defense mechanism. It gave me added joy to be able to say to Artie, "You were right! I was wrong. He's not dead."

Sometimes mothers know, and sometimes fathers know, and sometimes children know, and sometimes none of us knows, and that's the way life is, and we proceed together.

AS UNSETTLING OR AS COMFORTING as it may be, it seems the most enduring lessons conveyed to children come not through language but through gesture and example. The motion and stance of the body rarely lie. They almost always reveal the soul. Children are quick to detect hypocrisy and to resent it. They are just as quick to detect its opposite and are inclined to cooperate with that honesty.

I was in a fastfood restaurant recently, sitting near a family—mother, father, two sons around six and eight, and a baby girl. The father got up, carrying the trays of trash. The two boys went scrambling, running and pushing after him. One boy stumbled, the other boy tripped over him and fell into the dad. A sundae cup dropped off the tray, splattering melted ice cream all over the floor. The boys, sprawled on the floor, were laughing, wild, little darlings. The mother and dad looked resigned, like, "This is our life."

The dad and the two boys left and came back a moment later with napkins, and all three of them, the dad too, got down on the floor together and wiped up the ice cream. The boys were not scolded, not humiliated. There were no long lectures, yet the lesson was very clear: Men take responsibility for the consequences of their actions. Bless that dad.

This isn't a new thought—that actions speak louder than words—but it seems especially true in regard to children. Those intuitions and feelings of reverence that we call spiritual are communicated most genuinely to children through example.

My husband is fond of recalling an incident that occurred when he was young, a Boy Scout in Missouri. He was camping with his troop at Camp Osceola near the Osage River one summer night, inside his sleeping bag inside his tent. He remembers being awakened deep into the night by his scout master. He and the other boys were told to get up, not to talk, that they were all going somewhere. The scout master then led them through the forest of hardwoods, among the black trees steady with the stillness of night, up to a rock promontory high above the river and its valley.

It was clear and moonless. There were no trees on the rock bluff, and the entire night sky, completely filled with stars, was visible above them.

The boys lay down on the earth and watched the sky in silence. No one said anything. After a while, the scout master said it was time to go and led the boys back to their camp.

Recalling that night, my husband says that when he was previously inside his tent and in his sleeping bag, he felt he was defined, that he knew where he was and who he was. But when suddenly out beneath the night sky with its wide, descending history and moment of stars, he realized that he was part of something very much larger than his family, his troop, or this piece of ground in Missouri. He was part of the universe, part of something magnificent and beautiful and grand in its mystery.

Surely that scout master had faith both in the power of the universe to reveal itself and in the power and sensitivity of a boy to receive that revelation, and his faith was demonstrated in his action, communicated through the sacredness of his silence.

Divinity in the scout master's action, divinity in the stars in the sky in the night, in the boy, in human perception, divinity in the faith in divinity. May all parents possess similar faith.

Something good happens to the body and to perception when gratitude is expressed for the life we experience, not for life in general, but thanks for the particular form of life in the particular moment, because that is the most genuine and vibrant kind of thanks—for the gold of a low sun off the columbine by the fence, for the endurance of this old, tangled, apple tree with only one branch still living, for this child in my lap in this big chair by the window, for the bounding river, which is and is not, before me this very evening, which is and is not.

Gratitude expressed for the life of the moment bestows honor. Honor thus bestowed takes on the form and power of that specific life and returns to the giver the ability to forgive, to experience the expansive vision from which forgiveness of ourselves and others proceeds.

It is difficult to harbor hatred while walking at night across a snow-covered field, blue with the moon and its shadows, to remain resentful when surrounded by rocking summer grasses and coneflowers, a scatter of boulders rich with lichen. Jealousy and spite appear weak and ridiculous when seen against a sweeping world of currents and sky reflections, skating water striders, darters, minnows, the easy motion of mosses in the branching rootstocks beneath a pond lily.

We are not perfect people and neither are our children. But nature provides all the space and perspective we need to accept error, to create forgiveness. Honor and praise for our life, offered in whatever manner seems most efficacious—whether through literature or song, math or the visual arts, dance, the sciences, or simply through contemplation or an insightful question—is a form of prayer. During moments of such prayer, we might be able to move with a grace beyond ourselves. We must believe that our children will recognize this motion when it occurs and seek to emulate it in their own lives.

We can provide our children with opportunities to witness this prayer: in friends who love the earth, in musicians, artists, and writers who express our aspirations and our dilemmas, "the human heart in conflict with itself," in clowns and comedians who reveal our foolishness and pomposities, in scholars, scientists, and craftsmen whose passion and dedication to their work is evident, in other mothers and fathers and grandparents who give time and love to their children.

Some gestures of prayer may seem slight and transient at the time. Once on a cold March morning when I was a child, my mother called my brother and me excitedly to the window to see something in our backyard. I remember being disappointed that it was only a new cluster of purple crocus in bloom against the dead grasses. This whole incident took only a moment, and I am certain I must have uttered some remark like, "Is that all?" And yet my memory of this moment is vivid—my mother's delight, the reassurance in those brave first flowers of spring.

When our sons and daughters are grown, they might occasionally recall something of what we said to them during their childhoods, but it's certain they will always remember in their bodies how we lived, how we moved through time, the music and rhythms of our interactions within the family, within the society, within the natural world, what we valued, what we celebrated, how we encountered tragedy, how we defined failure and success. As adults, these memories will be as integral to them as their breath and pulse.

> Flesh of flesh
> Bone of my bone thou art and from thy state
> Mine never shall be parted, weal or woe.
> — John Milton, *The Eternal Bond*

WITHOUT SELF-RESPECT, it is difficult for any child or adult to understand how to respect the earth and other living beings. Without a sense of personal integrity, it is difficult for any child or adult to honor the integrity of the earth and those who live here with us. Without being loved with a love so steady and complete that its presence goes unnoticed, it is difficult for a child to know that such a love is possible or how to give a similar love to other human beings and to the life of the earth.

All people in all times have faced obstacles in their efforts to fulfill their obligations, to maintain their dignity and compassion, to live moral lives. Some have encountered more severe adversities than others—those, touched by wars and famines, extreme poverty, incurable diseases and epidemics, oppressive governments, disintegrating social structures. Within their particular circumstances all individuals have had to make difficult decisions in their attempts to live good and giving lives, often having to act counter to the popular notions of the time.

We are no different. We face our own challenges, those peculiar to our times and our individual circumstances. Today social and economic forces have put strains on the family and on many bonds that hold our communities together, and children have suffered as a result. I have seen them suffer myself—young children in schools where I have taught, children I have cared for, friends of my sons.

Children don't need an abundance of goods. They never have. They do need and deserve the enduring solicitude of both of their parents together, whenever at all possible, mother and father maintaining the family and sharing their children's history from birth through adulthood.

It hasn't been the fashion in recent years to keep promises, whether those promises were made publicly as in marriage vows, or whether those promises were implicit as those made to a baby conceived and brought into the world or to the earth upon which we depend. If we break faith with others, especially with our babies who are the embodiment of faith, what is to keep us from breaking faith with the earth as well?

If we will not take time from individual interests to be with our children and to create stable, loving homes where they can thrive, it seems unlikely that either we or our children will ever take the time or make the sacrifices necessary to insure the health and well-being of the earth, the first cradle and nurturing home of us all.

As we work to understand the concerns of raising children, how to proceed, desiring always the best future for the children we love and the earth we so revere, we know we can turn for strength to those things in the universe that we trust and from which we take comfort—perhaps the affirmation of life in the cellophane wings of a neon-blue dragonfly hovering mid-air, or the feel of someone loved close by in sleep, maybe the call of a cardinal and the subsequent discovery of his bright scarlet high in a winter oak, or the churning, boiling fright of the hot sun in the sky at noon, or the assertion in a gene of pollen flying from a blossom of wild strawberry—that elusive divinity as it comes to us and recedes from us in its myriad and glorious manifestations.

Stephanie Hanes

TODDLERS TO TWEENS
Relearning how to play

Children's play is threatened, say experts who advise that kids—from toddlers to tweens—should be relearning how to play. Roughhousing and fantasy feed development.

HAVELY TAYLOR KNOWS that her two children do not play the way she did when she was growing up. When Ms. Taylor was a girl, in a leafy suburb of Birmingham, Alabama, she climbed trees, played imaginary games with her friends, and transformed a hammock into a storm-tossed sea vessel. She even whittled bows and arrows from downed branches around the yard and had "wars" with friends—something she admits she'd probably freak out about if her children did it today. "I mean, you could put an eye out like that," she says with a laugh.

Her children—Ava, age 12, and Henry, 8—have had a different experience. They live in Baltimore, where Taylor works as an art teacher. Between school, homework, violin lessons, ice-skating, theater, and play dates, there is little time for the sort of freestyle play Taylor remembers. Besides, Taylor says, they live in the city, with a postage stamp of a backyard and the ever-present threat of urban danger. "I am kind of afraid to let them go out unsupervised in Baltimore...," she says, of how she started down this path with the kids. "I'm really a protective mom. There isn't much playing outside."

This difference has always bothered her, she says, because she believes that play is critical for children's developing emotions, creativity, and intelligence. So when she learned that her daughter's middle school had done away with recess, and even free time after lunch, she decided to start fighting for play. "It seemed almost cruel," she says. "Play is important for children—it's something so obvious it's almost hard to articulate. How can you talk about childhood without talking about play? It's almost as if they are trying to get rid of childhood."

Taylor joined a group of parents to pressure the principal to let their children have a recess, citing experts such as the U.S. Centers for Disease Control and Prevention, which recommends that all students have at least sixty minutes of physical activity every day. The parents issued petitions and held meetings. Although the school has not yet agreed to change its curriculum, Taylor says she feels their message is getting more recognition.

She is not alone in her concerns. In recent years, child development experts, parents, and scientists have been sounding an increasingly urgent alarm about the decreasing amount of time that children—and adults, for that matter—spend playing. A combination of social forces, from a No Child Left Behind focus on test scores to the push for children to get ahead with programmed extracurricular activities, leaves less time for the roughhousing, fantasizing, and pretend worlds that advocates say are crucial for development.

MEANWHILE, TECHNOLOGY and a wide-scale change in toys have shifted what happens when children do engage in leisure activity, in a way many experts say undermines long-term emotional and intellectual abilities. An 8-year-old today, for instance, is more likely to be playing with a toy that has a computer chip, or attending a tightly supervised soccer practice, than making up an imaginary game with friends in the backyard or street.

But play is making a comeback. Bolstered by a growing body of scientific research detailing the cognitive benefits of different types of play, parents like Taylor are pressuring school administrations to bring back recess and are fighting against a trend to move standardized testing and increased academic instruction into kindergarten.

Public officials are getting in on the effort. First Lady Michelle Obama and U.S. Secretary of Education Arne Duncan, for instance, have made a push for playgrounds nationwide. Local politicians from Baltimore to New York have participated in events such as the Ultimate Block Party—a metropolitan-wide play gathering. Meanwhile, business and corporate groups, worried about a future workforce hampered by a lack of creativity and innovations, support the effort. "It's at a tipping point," says Susan Magsamen, the director of Interdisciplinary Partnerships at the Johns Hopkins University School of Medicine Brain Science Institute, who has headed numerous child play efforts. "Parents are really anxious and really overextended. Teachers are feeling that way, too." So, when researchers say and can show that "it's OK to not be so scheduled [and] programmed— that time for a child to daydream is a good thing," Ms. Magsamen says, it confirms what families and educators "already knew, deep down, but didn't have the permission to act upon."

But play, it seems, isn't that simple. Scientists disagree about what sort of play is most important, government is loath to regulate the types of toys and technology that increasingly shape the play experience, and parents still feel pressure to supervise children's play rather than let them go off on their own. (Nearly two-thirds of Americans in a December Monitor TIPP poll, for instance, said it is irresponsible to let children play without supervision; almost as many said studying is more important than play.) And there is still pressure on schools to sacrifice playtime—often categorized as frivolous—in favor of lessons that boost standardized test scores. "Play is still terribly threatened," says Susan Linn, an instructor of psychiatry at Harvard Medical School and director of the nonprofit Campaign for a Commercial-Free Childhood. She adds, "What is changing is that there's a growing recognition that the erosion of play may be a problem ... we need to do something about."

One could say that the state of play, then, is at a crossroads. What happens to it—how it ends up fitting into American culture, who defines it, what it looks like—will have long-term implications for childhood, say those who study it. Some go even further. The future of play will define society overall and even determine the future of our species. "Play is the fundamental equation that makes us human," says Stuart Brown, the founder of the California-based National Institute for Play. "Its absence, in my opinion, is pathology."

Before advocates can launch a defense of play, they need to grapple with a surprisingly difficult question. What, exactly, is play? It might seem obvious. Parents know when their children are playing, whether it's a toddler scribbling on a piece of paper, an infant shaking a rattle, or a pair of 10-year-olds dressing up and pretending to be superheroes.

Can one define "play"? Even the *Merriam-Webster's Collegiate Dictionary* definition, "recreational activity; especially the spontaneous action of children," is often inaccurate, according to scientists and child development researchers. They say play for children is neither simply recreational nor necessarily spontaneous. "Play is when children are using something they've learned, to try it out and see how it works, to use it in new ways—it's problem solving and enjoying the satisfaction of problem solv[ed]," says Diane Levin, a professor of education at Wheelock College in Boston. Even in her class on the meaning and development of play, she never introduces one set definition. "This is something that people argue about," she says.

Scientists and child advocates agree that there are many forms of play. There is "attunement play," the sort of interaction where a mother and infant might gaze at each other and babble back and forth. There is "object play," where a person might manipulate a toy such as a set of marbles. There are "rough and tumble play" and "imaginative play." "Free play" is often described as kids playing on their own, without any adult supervision. "Guided play" is when a child or other player takes the lead, but a mentor is around to, say, help facilitate the Lego castle construction.

Often, says Dr. Brown at the National Institute for Play, a lot is happening all at once. He cites the time he tried to do a brain scan of his then 4-year-old grandson at play with his stuffed tiger. "He was clearly playing," Brown recalls. "And then he says to me, 'Grandpa, what does the tiger say?' I say, 'Roar!' And then he says, 'No, it says, "Moo!" ' and then laughs like crazy. How are you going to track that? He's pretending, he's making a joke, he's interacting."

This is one reason Brown says play has been discounted—both culturally and, until relatively recently, within the academic community, where detractors argue that play is so complex it cannot be considered one specific behavior, that it is an amalgamation of many different acts. These scientists—known as "play skeptics"—don't believe play can be responsible for all sorts of positive effects, in part because play itself is suspect. "It is so difficult to define and objectify," Brown notes. But most researchers agree that play clearly exists, even if it can't always be coded in the standard scientific way of other human behaviors. And the importance of play, Brown and others say, is huge.

Brown became interested in play as a young clinical psychiatrist when he was researching, somewhat incongruously, mass murderers. Although he concluded that many factors contributed to the psychosis of his subjects, Brown noticed that a common denominator was that none had participated in standard play behavior as children, such as interacting positively with parents or engaging in games with other children. As he continued his career, he took "play histories" of patients, eventually recording 6000. He saw a direct correlation between play behavior and happiness, from childhood into adulthood. It has a lot to do with joy, he says. "In the play studies, I'd find many adults who had a pretty playful childhood but then confined themselves to grinding, to always being responsible, always seeing just the next task. [They] are less flexible and have a chronic, smoldering depression. That lack of joyfulness gets to you."

Brown later worked with ethologists—scientists who study animal behavior—to observe how other species, from honeybees to Labrador retrievers, play. This behavior in a variety of species is sophisticated—from "self-handicapping," so a big dog can play fairly with a small dog, to cross-species play, such as a polar bear romping with a sled dog. He also studied research on play deprivation, noting how rat brains change negatively when they are deprived of some sorts of play. Brown became convinced that human play—for adults as well as children—is not only joyful but necessary, a behavior that is connected to the most ancient part of human biology and has survived despite connections in some studies to injury and danger (for example, animals continue to play even though they're likely to be hunted while doing so).

Other scientists are focusing on the specific impacts of play. In a small, brick testing room next to the "construction zone" at the Boston Children's Museum, for instance, Daniel Friel sits with a collection of brightly colored tubing glued to a board. The manager of the Early Childhood Cognition Lab in the Department of Brain and Cognitive Sciences at the Massachusetts Institute of Technology (MIT), he observes children at play with puppets and squeaky toys, rubber balls and fabulously created pipe sculptures. Depending on the experiment, Mr. Friel and other researchers record such data as the time a child plays with a particular object and what color ball is picked out of a container. These observations lead to insights on how children form their understanding of the world. "We are interested in exploratory play, how kids develop cause and effect, how they use evidence," he says.

The collection of tubing, for instance, is part of a study designed by researcher Elizabeth Bonawitz to test whether the way an object is presented can limit a child's exploration. If a teacher introduces the toy, which has a number of hidden points of interest—a mirror, a button that lights up, etc.—but tells a child about only one feature, the child is less likely to discover everything the toy can do than a child who receives the toy from a teacher who feigns ignorance. Without the instruction from an adult, it seems, a child is far more creative. In other words, adult hovering and instruction, from how to play soccer to how to build the best Lego city, can be limiting. Taken together, the MIT experiments show children calculating probabilities during play, developing assumptions about their physical environment, and adjusting perceptions according to the direction of authority figures. Other researchers are also discovering a breathtaking depth to play: how it develops chronological awareness and how it links to language development and self-control.

The latter point has been a hot topic recently. Self-regulation— the buzzword here is "executive function," referring to abilities such as planning, multitasking, and reasoning—may be more indicative of future academic success than IQ, standardized tests, or other assessments, according to a host of recent studies from institutions such as Pennsylvania State University and the University of British Columbia. Curriculums that boost executive function have become increasingly popular. Two years ago, Elizabeth Billings-Fouhy, director of the public Children's Place preschool in Lexington, MA, decided to adopt one such program, called Tools of the Mind. It was created by a pair of child development experts—Deborah Leong and Elena Bodrova—in the early 1990s after a study evaluating federal early literacy efforts found no positive outcomes.

"People started saying there must be something else," Dr. Leong says. "And we believed what was missing was self-regulation and executive function." She became interested in a body of research from Russia that showed children who played more had better self-regulation. This made sense to her, she says. For example, studies have shown that children can stand still far longer if they are playing soldier; other games such as Simon Says depend on concentration and rule-following. "Play is when kids regulate their behavior voluntarily," Leong says. Eventually, she and Dr. Bodrova developed the curriculum used today in the Children's Place, where students spend the day in different sorts of play. They act out long-form, make-believe scenes, they build their own props, and they participate in buddy reading, where one child has a picture of a pair of lips and the other has a picture of ears. The child with the lips reads, the other listens. Together, educators say, these various play exercises increase self-control.

This was on clear display recently at the Children's Place. Nearly half the children there have been labeled as special needs students with everything from autism to physical limitations. The others are mainstream preschoolers—an "easier" group, perhaps, but still not one typically renowned for its self-control. But in a brightly colored classroom, a group of 3-, 4-, and 5-year olds are notably calm, polite and quiet, sitting in pairs, taking turns "reading" a picture book. "Here are scissors, a brush ...," a boy named Aiden points out to his partner, Kyle, who is leaning in attentively.

"Oh, don't forget the paint," Kyle says, although he's mostly quiet, as it's his turn to listen.

Aiden nods and smiles: "Yes, the paint."

When Aiden is finished, the boys switch roles. Around them, another dozen toddlers do the same—all without teacher direction. The Tools classrooms have the reputation of being far better-behaved than mainstream classes. "We have been blown away," says Ms. Billings-Fouhy, the director, comparing how students are doing now versus before the Tools curriculum. "We can't believe the difference."

Educators and scientists have published overwhelmingly positive analyses since the early 2000s of the sort of curriculum Tools of the Mind employs. Recently the popularity of the play-based curriculum has skyrocketed, with more preschools adopting the Tools method and parenting chat rooms buzzing about the curriculum. Two years ago, for instance, Billings-Fouhy had to convince people about changing the Children's Place program. Now out-of-district parents call to get their children in.

"I think we're at this place where everyone is coming to the conclusion that play is important," Leong says. "Not just because of self-regulation, but because people are worried about the development of the whole child—their social and emotional development as well." Today's kids don't know how to play.

But not all play is created equal, experts warn. The Tools of the Mind curriculum, for instance, uses what Leong calls "intentional mature play"—play that is facilitated and guided by trained educators. If children in the class were told to simply go and play, she says, the result probably would be a combination of confusion, mayhem, and paralysis. "People say, 'Let's bring back play,' " Leong says. "But they don't realize play won't just appear spontaneously, especially not in preschool. ... The culture of childhood itself has changed."

For a host of reasons, today's children do not engage in all sorts of developmentally important play that prior generations automatically did.

In her class at Wheelock College, Levin has students interview people over the age of 50 about how they played. In the 1950s, and '60s, students regularly find, children played outdoors no matter where they lived, and without parental supervision. They played sports but adjusted the rules to fit the space and material—a goal in soccer, for instance, might be kicking a tennis ball to the right of the trashcan. They had few toys, and older children tended to act as "play mentors" to younger children, instructing them in the ways of make-believe games. That has changed dramatically, she says. In the early 1980s, the federal government deregulated children's advertising, allowing TV shows to essentially become half-hour-long advertisements for toys such as Power Rangers, My Little Ponies, and Teenage Mutant Ninja Turtles. Levin says that's when children's play changed. They wanted specific toys and to use them in the specific ways that the toys appeared on TV.

Today, she says, children are "second generation deregulation," and not only have more toys—mostly media-based—but also lots of screens. A Kaiser Family Foundation study recently found that 8- to 18-year-olds spend an average of 7.5 hours in front of a screen every day, with many of those hours involving multiscreen multitasking. Toys for younger children tend to have reaction-based operations, such as push-buttons and flashing lights. Take away the gadgets and the media-based scripts, Levin and others say, and many children today simply don't know what to do. "If they don't have the toys, they don't know how to play," she says.

The American educational system, increasingly teaching to standardized tests, has also diminished children's creativity, says Kathy Hirsh-Pasek, a professor of psychology and director of the Infant Language Laboratory at Temple University in Philadelphia. "Children learn from being actively engaged in meaningful activities," she says. "What we're doing seems to be the antithesis of this. We're building robots. And you know, computers are better robots than children." Other countries, particularly in Asia, she notes, have already shifted their educational focus away from test scores, and Finland—which is at the top of international ranking—has a policy of recess after every class for Grades 1 through 9.

But, as Dr. Hirsh-Pasek points out, children spend most of their time out of school. A playful life is possible if parents and communities know what to do. The Ultimate Block Party, which Hirsh-Pasek developed with other researchers, is one way to involve local governments, educators, and institutions in restoring play and creativity, she says. The Ultimate Block Party is a series of play stations—from blocks and sandboxes to dress-up games and make-believe environments—where kids can play with their parents. Meanwhile, the event's staff helps explain to caregivers what sorts of developmental benefits the children achieve through different types of play.

The first Ultimate Block Party in New York's Central Park in October 2010 attracted 50,000 people; Toronto and Baltimore held parties last year. Organizers now say they get multiple requests from cities every month to hold their own block parties; Hirsh-Pasek says she hopes the movement will go grassroots, with towns and neighborhoods holding their own play festivities. "It's an exciting time," she says. "We're starting to make some headway. It's time for all of us to find the way to become a more creative, thinking—culture."

Carolyn Jabs

THE PRIVILEGE OF GARDENING WITH CHILDREN

LAST WEEKEND my son and I planted peas. When we went to the hardware store to buy seeds, he studied the seed rack earnestly. At 3½, he couldn't read but he knows his pictures, and he was adamant when he spotted his favorites. I tried to add a package of snap peas but he couldn't be fooled. "The ones that come out of the pods," he insisted. So we bought two packages of very early Lancaster peas and drove home.

Our garden doesn't seem very big to me. And when we moved to New Hampshire in the early eighties, I quickly understood why all the serious farmers had moved west one hundred fifty years ago. Even after three rounds of rock picking, our small plot is strewn with gravel and worse. Despite my conscientious applications of manure and mulch, the black layer of fertile earth seems discouragingly thin.

None of this matters to my son. He carried his packets of seeds as if they were a treasure, which, I suppose, they were. And he waited impatiently for me to turn over a few rows at the less sodden end of the garden. After I made a shallow furrow about ten feet long, he asked me to open one of the packets and then stood in front of me, grubby palm upturned, waiting for a handful of seeds.

At first he planted them side by side, but when I explained that they needed room to grow, he showed an unexpected ability to place the seeds at regular two-inch intervals. Soon a little dotted line ran from one end of the furrow to the other and he announced that he was all done. "What about covering the seeds?" I asked. And I stooped down to show him how to spread the soil over the furrow and pat it down. In a moment, my son was kneeling beside me, gently smoothing the soil and saying softly, "Good night, seeds!"

You can never be sure just what children are learning from the experiences you offer them, but in that moment I was certain my son understood the difference between the seeds he'd just planted and the pebbles he collects with such zeal. He had grasped, somehow, that these seeds would "awaken" after he tucked them in, and he was treating them with all the tenderness that living things deserve.

I invited my son into the garden because I thought he would learn a lot about the cycles of nature, the sources of food, the rewards of hard work. Apparently he is learning some of those things. Yet, as so often happens, I'm the real beneficiary. As adults, we tend to become fixated on results in and out of the garden. I get frustrated by the size of my stony garden, vengeful toward the pests that plague it, cross about the weeds that compete with my crops. Children, on the other hand, have a deep and abiding interest in growing, perhaps because they are doing it themselves. They remind us, if we let them, that the point of gardening is not a perfect platoon of well-disciplined plants. Rather, it is the privilege of witnessing a miracle as simple, profound, and unpredictable as growth itself.

AMONG OTHER THINGS, gardening with children gives parents a chance to register changes in them that might otherwise go unnoticed. When a child is very young, the garden will be, above all, a place for dabbling in the dirt, something that American children don't get much opportunity to do. My son's first gardening experience came at 18 months when he solemnly filled (and emptied) little peat pots with sterile potting soil. By the following year, he'd lost interest in filling and dumping but was obsessed with the garden hose and wanted to water everything (including his parents). This year he's intrigued by the seeds themselves.

At this stage, it might be time to give him a garden of his own. Lots of experts recommend it, to help develop a sense of ownership. It's also a way of heading off conflict between parent and child. If you're going to be distressed every time your child steps on a cucumber vine or picks a flower off the tomatoes, by all means make your garden off-limits and assign him or her a separate plot. On the other hand, some children develop a sense of respect for plants. Even at 2½, my son could navigate among the fragile young seedlings, and when in doubt, he'd ask, "Can I step here, Mommy?"

In her book, *Earthly Delights*, Rosalind Creasy writes about how she was given her own garden under an apple tree when she was four or five years old. "I treated my garden much as I did my doll house, as something that needed constant rearranging." She recalls, "I seldom produced anything, and most of my plants died because they were weary from being moved ... I was told: 'You must not move your carrots.' Instead, I moved my carrots and discovered that, instead of straight, succulent carrots, I got 'many gnarled things,' multi-pointed corkscrews."

Openness to children's decisions—and discoveries—in the garden is an attitude most parents must cultivate. Too often we recruit children to carry out our plans. We, after all, know when and how things should be planted, weeded, and watered. Yet, if we turn our children into little foot soldiers, they are likely to become resentful of what seems to be just another chore. Instead of rushing out to the garden to learn the latest results of their collaboration with nature, they'll drag their feet, dreading a new assignment that has meaning to grown-ups but not to them.

TO FIND OUT WHAT'S meaningful to your child, you have to ask—and listen—to the answers. For instance, many books recommend that children plant radishes, which is fine if your child likes radishes. Personally, I don't know why they do, although some get a certain satisfaction out of pulling the little red balls from the ground. In general, children are more likely to be enthusiastic about the garden if it produces things that are appealing, either because they like to eat them or because they are curious about how they grow.

Radishes are usually recommended because they grow fast. Yet, in the garden, speed isn't the point. Nature teaches all of us that some things can't be hurried, a lesson that's particularly valuable in our fast-forward world. Last spring my son planted his first peas on a Sunday afternoon. On

Monday morning, he headed for the garden as soon as he was outdoors. When he saw that there was nothing but dirt, he began to wail. "Peas," he cried, "Peas, peas, peas." I know he didn't believe me that day when I told him that the peas would eventually grow. He was still doubtful when two wavy, green lines appeared where he had tucked the seeds into the ground. And he was equally skeptical when I insisted that the white flowers would turn into peas. But one day he could see that there were tiny pea pods under each flower, and this year he planted his crop, secure in his faith that the peas will grow in their own time.

Older children often have definite ideas about what should go into their gardens. One may decide to grow fennel because the name sounds funny, or purple broccoli because purple is her favorite color, or pumpkins because he wants one for Halloween. Indulge these whims. A child's garden is no place for insisting that this or that be grown "because it's good for you." Children tend to eat what they've grown because they've grown it, and in the process they discover that truly fresh vegetables taste terrific. It takes restraint to let the vegetables speak on their own behalf, but parents who do are likely to be surprised by the enthusiasm with which their children embrace broccoli, beets, and beans.

To help your child make choices, page through a colorfully illustrated seed catalog together. Older children can cut out pictures of the vegetables they've ordered to make a garden scrapbook. Later the child can record details about when the seeds were planted, how long it took for the seedlings to appear, when the crop was ready for harvest, how it tasted, and so on. For younger children, browsing through catalogs is more an opportunity to learn the names and colors of various vegetables and flowers. Actually ordering by mail may try the patience of children under 6. At that age, it's better to get up one sunny spring morning, go the farm supply store, pick your seeds off the rack, and take them straight home to be planted.

Although your child should select the type of vegetable whenever possible, you can head off some problems by carefully choosing the variety. For instance, check maturity dates so you can plan around the family vacation or your child's week at camp. Nothing is more disappointing than tending two rows of beans only to have them all ripen when everyone is away. Also, whenever possible, look for varieties that will resist local pests and diseases. Children often like to eat their produce right from the garden, an inclination you can encourage if you haven't used pesticides and other chemicals.

When you're choosing varieties, remember that miniature vegetables are as appealing to children as they are to adults. Even if you don't have a yard, children can plant minis in containers and still have a fine harvest on a terrace or windowsill. Lilliputian vegetables fit more easily, not only into children's gardens, but also into hands and mouths. Try cherry tomatoes— Sweet 100 produces hundreds of marble-sized tomatoes—baseball-sized watermelons, baby beets, and even egg-sized eggplants.

If your child is too young to have definite preferences about what he or she will grow, you can't go wrong with peas and beans. Some of my best moments in the garden have been spent raiding the pea patch with my son. We almost never get enough for a meal because we shell them and eat them on the spot, an indulgence I justify by telling myself that they are sweetest—and most nutritious—straight from the vine. If your child's likes and dislikes aren't as fixed as my son's, you can also suggest sugar and snow peas. Dwarf varieties are child-sized and spare you the labor of building a trellis for the plants to climb. Although peas take up quite a bit of space for what they yield, they can be planted enough in most climates to allow a second crop of something more prolific on the same ground.

Beans can't be planted until after the last frost. If you're gardening with a child, don't limit yourself to the green bush beans. Instead try Royal Burgundy that has purple pods (they turn green when cooked) or yellow beans (don't call them wax—it makes them sound as though they'll taste dreadful). It's also worth the effort to grow pole beans, if only to make *Jack and the Beanstalk* come alive. Some of the old varieties such as Jacob's Cattle or Missouri Wonder have seeds with such beautiful colors and patterns that they can easily be considered "magic." Pole beans are practical too because the beans ripen gradually from the bottom of the vine to the top. Most children will be tickled to sit on a parent's shoulders and pick the beans at the top of the pole.

To make the bean patch even more inviting, lash the ends of six poles together to make a teepee. If you don't have access to the traditional saplings, 1x2s from the lumberyard will do. They should be seven or eight feet tall. Then spread the other ends to make a circle with a three-foot diameter and anchor the poles in the dirt. Plant four to six beans at the base of each pole—consider a variety with brilliant flowers like Scarlet Runner. Mulch the inside of the teepee with straw. As the beans twine up the poles, they'll create a secret space that will enchant most children.

Carrots are a good choice for a child's first crop, though the seeds are so small that you shouldn't even try to sow them. Instead, mark out a square and let your child broadcast the seeds into it. If you're determined to have long carrots, you'll probably need to mix sand into your soil. Children, however, are just as happy with the stubby varieties that can wedge their way through almost anything. Also, the shorter carrots are less likely to break off when pulled. When it's time to harvest, show your child how to grasp the greens right above the carrot's shoulders.

Actually, anything that grows underground is astonishing for a child. Try raising some beets and even parsnips or turnips. By all means, start a potato patch. Children are amused by the idea of a vegetable that has "eyes," and a spud that's sprouted looks like a Dr. Seuss creature. If you plant your potatoes in furrows and then mulch them with straw, you and your child can forget about them until late summer. Then go treasure hunting. Few things are as satisfying to young or old gardeners as turning over a spadeful of dirt to reveal a cache of new potatoes. For even more suspense, try planting potatoes of different colors—red, blue, and even purple are available.

No child's garden would be complete without a pumpkin patch. Even if you don't raise other vegetables, designate a forgotten corner of the yard for a pumpkin vine. Help your child make a mound of earth mixed with compost or rotted manure. Smooth the top and poke in four seeds.

If you want a giant pumpkin, pull all out but one plant. After it sets one pumpkin, pick off subsequent flowers so all the energy goes into producing one humongous pumpkin. Challenging as it may be to raise a pumpkin so big that no one can carry it, children often prefer to grow several smaller specimens so they can give them to friends for jack-o'-lanterns. To monogram a special pumpkin for a child, scratch his or her name into the young fruit with the tip of a knife.

At the back of the garden, be sure to include a row of sunflowers—the bigger the better. In her book, *Gardening with Kids*, Sharon MacLatchie writes that the towering sunflowers always inspired imagination games with her son. "Giant flowers, giant insects, apples the size of basketballs, treetops invisible through the clouds," she writes. "What would happen if our relative size were to drastically change? Children's answers are fascinating; after all, theirs by comparison is a small world." Ask them. Of course, sunflower seeds make a nutritious snack, not only for the children but also for the birds. Try hanging one of the seed heads from a tree branch to make a swinging feeder for the chickadees.

After you've had success with some of the tried-and-true crops, experiment with some that are more unusual. Try raising watermelons—be sure to match the variety to the length of the growing season. In warmer climates, plant some peanuts—their growing habits are sure to provoke conversation. Or plant a few gourds. Though they aren't edible, children enjoy turning them into dippers, rattles, boxes, and birdhouses. If your child has a cat, put in a patch of catnip. If your garden is large enough, consider a small block of popcorn. Or add a border of Alpine strawberries, a perennial that bears tiny, tasty berries all summer long. Don't attempt all these novelties in one season, but make a point of trying something new every year.

In your enthusiasm for edibles, don't neglect flowers. Children who have been warned not to touch the prize specimens in the cutting garden will revel in a plot where they can pick as they please for impromptu presentations to parents, friends, or teachers. For young children, be sure the flowers are big and bright—flaming red salvia, cheery marigolds, brassy zinnias. Don't forget snapdragons—no child can resist snapping them. Older children may also enjoy flowers such as strawflowers, Chinese lanterns, baby's breath, and luminaria that can be dried and used in winter crafts.

HAVING CHOSEN WHAT SHOULD go into the garden, you and your child are ready to plant. Before you start, impress upon young children that they must never put seeds in their mouths; some are treated with fungicides and other harmful chemicals. In planting, as in other gardening activities, respect your young child's attention span. Better to put in a row of beans today and a patch of pumpkins tomorrow than exhaust everyone's patience in one marathon session. While you plant, talk to your child about the sizes, shapes and colors of different seeds. Save a few from each vegetable in the compartments of an egg carton. An older child might want to look at a seed under a magnifying glass or split it open to see what's inside.

To hold children's interest during the dull days between planting and sprouting, germinate some seeds in a jar so they can see what's going on underground. The simplest way to do this is to line the inside of a straight-sided jar with blotting paper (construction paper is an adequate substitute) and stuff the inside with paper towels. Slip the seeds between the paper and the jar. Then keep the paper towels damp and take a look every day or so to see what's happening. In this and in other activities, don't spoil the suspense by telling your child what to expect. Wait and watch together.

Once the garden is planted, mulch wherever possible to keep down weeds. Very young children won't be able to distinguish between desirable and undesirable plants, but they will be able to make little mounds of straw between rows. Even older children who can tell a carrot from a blade of grass may not have the dexterity to pull out one without injuring the other. Better that you should do the weeding while your child does some sort of companionable task nearby. For instance, when I hoe, my son takes it upon himself to relocate the worms that I uncover. I hand them to him and he gently carries them to an undisturbed part of the garden.

Older children who have their own gardens should be encouraged to tend them, mostly by example. If they see that you can find your tomatoes because you've weeded around them, they may want a comparable look in their spaces. On the other hand, don't impose your own standards for tidiness on their patches. Many vegetables compete reasonably well with weeds, and few things will kill a young gardener's enthusiasm as quickly as mandatory weeding.

One way to spark children's interest in maintaining a garden is to equip them with good, serviceable tools. Plastic ones are a waste of money; children will simply be frustrated because they can't do what they see you're doing. Instead, invest in a quality trowel and consider cutting down the handle of one of your hoes. If your child shows a real zeal for gardening, first-rate child-sized tools are available from suppliers.

When it comes right down to it, weeding is one of the few gardening chores children resist. Most love to water. If possible, locate the garden so that it can be reached by the garden hose. A filled watering can is too heavy for a young child to carry and smaller containers are half empty by the time they reach the garden. If you set the hose on dribble or mist, your child can give plants a drink without drowning them.

Harvesting is another "chore" that won't seem laborious to a child. This is the kind of work in which the rewards are instantly apparent. The memory of eating tiny new beans or sun-warmed tomatoes straight from the vine is often enough to send a child back into the garden the following spring. Just remember that once children have gotten the habit of eating off the land, they may be tempted to sample things that look edible on other plants. Since many wild plants are poisonous, be sure children understand that they should ask before tasting anything outside the garden.

To adults who have to keep up with the weeding while picking and processing the bounty, the late summer garden may seem to be nothing more than a succession of chores. Of course, more than half the work is being done by the plants, so take some time to point out their contributions to your child. Be aware of when each species flowers and how the flower transforms itself into fruit. Talk about how the plants are affected by the weather you've been having. No matter what chores remain undone, spend some time simply walking in the garden, feeling the warm massage of the sun on your back, the potent smells of earth that's been cultivated, the pressure of your child's hand in yours.

Pay attention to the wildlife, too. For a child, a stroll through the garden can be like a trip to a miniature zoo. Often large animals will be visible only through the clues they leave behind, forcing you and your child to play detective. Who could have gnawed on the carrot, ransacked the corn, nibbled on the lettuce? The creatures you can observe firsthand are likely to be lowlier—earthworms and hornworms, bean beetles and cabbage butterflies. For parents, this may require some self-control, particularly if you come from a swat-and-spray school of entomology. Try to conquer your own prejudices and approach each living thing with your child's open-minded curiosity.

Last summer when a large slug chewed all three of our pumpkin plants down to the stem, my son was sad about the pumpkins but intrigued by the slug. Why didn't it have legs? Where did it live? Why did it eat his pumpkins? Answer your child's questions and ask some, too. They're likely to listen more closely to your answers if you don't always know what they are: Why do you think centipedes have so many legs? Why do hornworms like to eat tomatoes and not zucchini?

IF ALL OF THIS MAKES gardening with children sound too idyllic to be true, you're right. Certainly there will be moments when your child gathers all the squash blossoms to make you a bouquet, "thins" the lettuce after seeing you do it, or stands at the edge of the garden, whining and bored, while you beg for time to put in onions, weed the beans, or pick the broccoli. Perhaps because they are difficult, those moments are also an opportunity for you to join your child and your plants in growing. Stretch your thinking until you can see those squash blossoms as your child did—the most beautiful thing that he or she could give to you. Expand your heart until you feel the honor implicit in your child's desire to be just like you and do the things you do. Reach with your arms to hug the child who needs your attention every bit as much as your plants do. When you invite your child into the garden, the most important thing you can cultivate is your relationship.

James E. Higgins

WORDS FULL OF WONDER

*Never say there is nothing beautiful in the world anymore. There
is always something to make you wonder in the shape of a tree, the
trembling of a leaf.*

– Albert Einstein
For All That Lives

THE REALIZATION THAT disaster lurks ahead unless humans make
changes in their relation to the natural order has spurred a new interest
in environmental education. It will be a tragic oversight, however, if new
education programs emphasize only scientific information and reason, with
a bit of evangelizing thrown in. The humanities have an equal contribution
to make, specifically that branch called literature and more particularly
children's literature. *Charlotte's Web*, for instance, has changed more
people's behavior toward spiders than any scientific text I know.

As I hope to show, a nature connection is ever present in the
preponderance of literary works for children. Nature, after all, is the
writer's only source for material representation that has an infinite
constancy. Many of the best storytellers and poets have learned to "read"
nature themselves and then turned what they read there into words. For
the audience of their stories and poems, the process is reversed: We read
and listen to the words, then look out at the natural world that inspired
them, often to see it in a way that is refreshingly new and significant.

Stories and poems, when they do their work, have the power to
educe from readers or listeners, young or old, feelings of wonder and awe
concerning nature and their own place in it. These feelings are not merely

emotional responses, but the very basis of aesthetic, metaphorical thinking. The good writer goes not back to childhood, but down into childhood, to uncover the mythopoeic essence of experience. He calls upon the child within himself to intensify sensation so that he can recreate a moment of simple wonder: the white streaks of snow as they pass through the light of the street lamp, the loveliness of suckling a newborn pup, the fright of waiting for the next clap of thunder to shake the house.

Children have the capacity to grasp this essence, even though they may not understand it nor be able to express the feeling it engenders. In his autobiographical work, *Surprised by Joy*, C.S. Lewis remembers that even before he could read, he was strongly moved by Beatrice Potter's *Squirrel Nutkin*. It was not, in his words,

> ...merely entertaining; it administered the shock, it was a trouble. It troubled me with what I can only describe as the Idea of Autumn. It sounds fantastic to say that one can be enamored of a season, but that is something like what happened;... the experience was one of intense desire. And one went back to the book, not to gratify the desire (that was impossible—how can one possess Autumn) but to reawake it. And in this experience also there was the same surprise and the same incalculable importance. It was something quite different from ordinary life and even from ordinary pleasure, something as they now say, "in another dimension."

Lewis knew, as we all should know, that a profound feeling for nature is not beyond the ken of children.

Since I am writing these words in the time of autumn, let me give a few more examples of how some other authors have evoked an autumnal feeling in works for children, thereby touching off sensations of wonder in listeners and readers.

Frederick by Leo Lionni is a picture book that opens in that special moment of autumn when first comes the chilly portent of approaching winter. Frederick and his family of field mice live in an old stone wall, not far from a barn and granary. "But the farmer had moved away, the barn was abandoned, and the granary stood empty. And since winter was not far off, the little mice began to gather corn and nuts and wheat and straw. They had all worked day and night. All—except Frederick."

For Frederick, as we are told on the last pages of the book, is the poet of the group. It is his job to gather other necessities to help see the family through the winter:

> sun rays – to warm them on cold winter days
> color – for winter is gray
> words – so that they won't run out of things to say

Another example of autumn feeling is found in Chapter 8 of *Bambi* by Felix Salten. This three-page gem of a chapter, which has no plot connection with the story, is inserted explicitly to prepare the reader/listener for the dark, cold atmosphere of approaching winter and the stark reality it signifies for the animals of the forest. It opens with the sentence: "The leaves were falling from the great oak at the meadow's edge." Clinging precariously to their hold, they carry on a conversation in which they wonder and share their fears about what will happen to them after they have fallen. Salten avoids sentimentality; the conversation breaks off abruptly when one leaf is in the middle of a comment: "She was torn from her place and spun down. Winter had come." (It is a pity that so many people have accepted the Disney film, or short book adaptations from the film, in place of the original Salten novel, which is truly a classic, not to be missed.)

My final example of autumn feeling is from another classic. In the final conversation before her death, Charlotte, the spider in *Charlotte's Web*, perhaps the greatest of all heroines in children's literature, tells Wilbur the pig that she feels

> a little tired perhaps. But I feel peaceful. ...Your future is assured. You will live, secure and safe, Wilbur. Nothing can

harm you now. These autumn days will shorten and grow cold. The leaves will shake loose from the trees and fall. Christmas will come, then the snows of winter. You will live to enjoy the beauty of the frozen world. ...Winter will pass, the days will lengthen, the ice will melt in the pasture pond. The song sparrow will sing, the frogs will awake, the warm wind will blow again. All these sights and sounds and smells will be yours to enjoy. Wilbur—this lovely world, these precious days...

If you have never had the occasion to share this American masterpiece with a child, do yourself a favor and go do it. You will see that the words such as the ones above are not wasted on children; they are, in fact, the audience best attuned to the inner resonance of the telling. We adults are the lucky ones in such an encounter, though, because the reverent intensity with which the child attends to the words has a way of reverberating back to us with a freshness and newness that do not often come our way.

TAKE ANY ONE OF the hundreds of natural objects and you will find them powerfully represented in even the simplest literary works for children. The adult who is reading has only to recognize the power of the language and then exploit it through his genuine participation in the experience of the words. As I point out to children who can read, stories and poems are put into books so that we can preserve them, but they cannot live unless we resurrect them from the silence of the printed page and breathe life back into them with our voices, our minds, and our hearts. For a test, just pick up one of the stories from *The Jungle Book* by Rudyard Kipling and see what a difference it makes to hear the words as you read, even if the sound is "inside" you.

Reading aloud is only part of what I am talking about. From the very beginning, I want children to experience story and poetry as children always have and still do in societies that have no access to the written word. Stories and poems have traditionally been a part of ritual—a way of creating an occasion, taking an everyday occurrence and making it something special and personal. Used in this manner, words are alive with sound, dynamic with immediacy, and a means for children to connect their inside world with the world around them.

To illustrate, let me select one of my favorite subjects—stars. Since I spend much of my time with city children, stars are often the most accessible form of nature, calling out to each of them, "You there, look up!" Frequently when I speak to groups of parents of young children, I have them recite along with me the simple little rhyme with which they are all familiar:

> Twinkle, twinkle, little star,
> How I wonder what you are,
> Up above the world so high
> Like a diamond in the sky.

Most parents proudly report that not only do their children know the verse, but it was they who taught them. When I ask how they taught them and how the children learned, they generally reply that it was through repetition, sometimes mistakenly called "learning by heart"—the heart really has little to do with it. To be sure, it is a legitimate mode of learning, and for a lifetime the words of the rhyme will remain in the head, ready for automatic recall.

How different a language experience it might be, however, if the adult were to take the child out into a starlit night so that the two of them might look and wonder together. A conversation might begin with the parent saying something like this: "Do you see that one way over there?—that's my special star. I'll share it with you. Or maybe you'd like to pick out your own." After the exciting ritual of choosing is over, both of them address their particular stars and chant the magic words, "Twinkle, twinkle..." How much more mysterious, more intense, are the words now. And stars forever are put into the child's "wondering" inventory. The quality of simple belief that the adult brings to such an encounter, of course, will determine the genuineness of the child's own belief. For belief, or making believe, is what such play is all about. Fortunate the adult who can still look up at the stars, recite the rhyme, and re-experience the initial wonder.

Many authors unabashedly invite their audience to join them in imaginary conversations with the stars, and children, for their part, will most often eagerly accept the invitation, especially if the adult reader enters into the spirit of the story. Antoine de Saint-Exupéry was one such author. Underlying all of this famous Frenchman's writings, whether aviation adventures or philosophical musings, is his fascination with the stars. It is also at the very heart of his final work, the children's classic *The Little Prince*, completed during World War II shortly before he disappeared on a reconnaissance flight. At the conclusion of the story, just before the Little Prince departs from Earth to return to his tiny planet, he consoles the aviator-narrator by leaving him a gift:

> All men have the stars ... but you—you alone will have the stars as no one else has them...

> In one of the stars I shall be living. In one of them I shall be laughing. And so it will be as if all the stars were laughing, when you look up at the sky at night...

> It will be as if, in place of stars, I have given you a great number of little bells that know how to laugh.

The physical act of looking up at the stars is often an occasion for expressing one's innermost thoughts. Stars have always had a strong connection with the meditative or prayerful act of wishing. We find it in the simplest of rhymes:

> Star light, star bright,
> First star I see tonight,
> I wish I may, I wish I might,
> Have the wish I wish tonight.

Or the familiar lyrics from the cricket's song in the film *Pinocchio*: "When you wish upon a star..." Or in the little poem by Sara Teasdale titled "Falling Star":

> I saw a star slide down the sky,
> Blinding the north as it went by,
> Too burning and too quick to hold,
> Too lovely to be bought or sold,
> Good only to make wishes on
> And then forever to be gone.

In some stories, such wishes are encouraged through the thought that they will not go unheard. Stars are major presences in William Steig's books for children. In picture books like *Sylvester and the Magic Pebble*, *Amos and Boris*, and *Gorky Rises*, exquisite two-page layouts of finely drawn illustrations depict vast, luminous, star-filled skies. The texts reveal Steig's own wonder concerning the plight of small, seemingly helpless, earthbound creatures in the immense cosmos. His work is completely in tune with children's wonderings about themselves and the world. Without any preaching, without a heavy hand, he subtly suggests the possibility that there may be good cause for wonder: that perhaps there is a force within the vast universe that is aware of the troubles and predicaments in which even the smallest of creatures find themselves.

In Steig's books for older children, too, stars play an important role. In *Abel's Island*, a fantasy, the mouse Abel is suddenly stranded on an island, cut off from everything, including his new bride, Amanda. Abel's story is very similar in many ways to realistic stories of castaways like Crusoe and like the Indian girl Karana in Scott O'Dell's *The Island of the Blue Dolphins*, in that Abel must not only fight off physical enemies and protect himself from the severity of the elements, but he must resist spiritual despair. At one point, when his spirits are at their lowest, he turns his gaze to the sky.

He was suddenly thrilled to see his private, personal star arise in the east. This was a particular star his nanny had chosen for him when he was a child. As a child, he would sometimes talk to this star, but only when he was his most serious, real self, and not being any sort of a show-off or clown. As he grew up, the practice had somehow worn off.

He looked up at his old friend as if to say, "You see my predicament."

The star seemed to respond, "I see."

Abel next put the question: "What shall I do?"

The star seemed to answer. "You will do what you will do." For some reason this reply strengthened Abel's belief in himself. Sleep gently enfolded him. The constellations proceeded across the hushed heavens as if tiptoeing past the dreaming mouse on his high branch.

Certain stars have served as symbolic centers for powerful stories in history and legend. For instance, since the time it beckoned Harriet Tubman and her entourage of runaway slaves to freedom, the North Star has had deep spiritual significance for Black Americans. One of the books that celebrates this association is *North Star Rising* by Hildegarde Swift, with illustrations by Lynd Ward. And of course, there is the story of the Star of Bethlehem, first told in the Gospel of St. Matthew, and still commemorated worldwide every year in poetry, song, and story.

In many places in the world, as I mentioned earlier, adult storytellers still enchant children with homespun stories. Some of these emerge from a long tradition of the clan or tribe. Today they can be found in many anthologies. For stories of stars, for instance, we can go to the collections of constellation myths such as *The Stars Are Silver Reindeer* by Natalie Belting and *The Heavenly Zoo* by Alison Lurie. Other tales, however, are not part of any tradition but arise extemporaneously to meet some immediate or unexpected need for instruction or consolation. Sad to say, this particular type of story is rarely utilized in industrialized societies. Nevertheless, its potential is ever present.

A story about a star that appeared some years ago in the *New York Daily News* demonstrated the power a simple extemporaneous story that springs from the heart can have in people's lives. Greta-Jean Joliff, a woman in her early forties, had written the newspaper article from her home in England to help her find two United States servicemen whom she had known as an 8-year old girl during World War II. She had little information about the men, not even their names. She had been evacuated from London in 1941 to a camp where children were cared for by American GIs. While she was there she learned that her mother had been killed in the Blitz. One of the soldiers, to comfort her, had told her a story at bedtime. In the story, all lovers had secret stars, so of course her mother would come down the beam so that they could be together. In her letter, Greta-Jean wrote that she still looked up to the stars at night and smiled as she remembered the story. Though all of the other details of the incident had blurred, the story remained vivid, and its consoling effect constant.

THE EXAMPLES I HAVE selected up until this point have been chosen from material that would not necessarily be considered "nature" literature, or valued for its nature content. Too often, the natural objects that appear in literature—stars and trees and ponds and rocks—are treated in literature classes as mere symbols and are linguistically denatured in the process. Such treatment literally draws the life out of the object and reduces the representative words to flat prose and the reader to an objective observer of, rather than an active participant in, the unfolding story or poem. This positivistic approach to literature not only obscures any nature content of a story or poem, but also automatically excludes young children from what might be called literary experiences, for it is argued, and with good reason, that such experiences are beyond their intellectual capabilities. (Indeed I think this approach is also what bores the pants off their older brothers and sisters in literature classes, and causes them to find little connection between what they read and what they see in the world around them.)

For the child, star, tree, pond, and rock are symbols, but symbols in the true sense: They transcend intellectual decoding, they defy explanation, summation, and closure. Rather, they awaken feelings from deep within and urge even the youngest participant to *play out* such a meaning. The child is sufficiently prepared, perhaps better so than adults, for such linguistic excursions. He is totally open to newness, since almost everything is new to him. He has tolerance for mystery, since almost everything for him is tinged with mystery. Above all, he has the spontaneity, the energy, and the capacity for belief that are so necessary for play—perhaps the highest form of human endeavor. As Chesterton points out, "The man writing on motherhood is merely an educationalist. The child playing with a doll is a mother."

Such play, as I have tried to show, does not depend on language skills so much as on an awareness that comes through the use of the senses. The senses are the most powerful means for awakening the imagination. Yet their training has had little part in the process of education. In fact, the word "sense" itself has taken up an almost abstract meaning; if one says, "I'll bring him to his senses," one most often means, "I'll bring him to reason."

Some of the best writers of literature for children understand very well how to awaken the child's ability to sense the world around him. I think, for instance, of the works of Byrd Baylor. Baylor is a one-of-a-kind writer; her books cannot readily be classified. She is a native of the Southwest and her writing reflects her great love for that locale and the people who live there, particularly Native Americans. Yet the appeal of her work is universal, as this writer, a 60-year-old child of the city can attest.

The Other Way to Listen by Baylor is a great book for sharing with children, and a good example of one that invites readers and listeners to use their senses to explore their surroundings. It isn't a story in the usual meaning of the word. In it an Indian boy of the Southwest speaks directly to the reader/listener. He relates some of his experiences and conversations with an old man, who instructs him in the "other way to listen." This is the kind of listening that allows one to hear "wildflower seeds burst open, beginning to grow underground" or "a cactus blooming in the dark" or "a whole sky full of stars."

The boy finds out that this kind of listening is learned from "the hills and ants and lizards and weeds and things like that." They do the teaching. One of the secrets imparted by the old man is that people must not be ashamed to learn from bugs or sand or anything. He admonishes the boy: "If you think you're *better* than a horned toad, you'll never hear its voice." The boy finds that learning to listen in this way is not as difficult as it seemed at first. In fact, it's really "the most natural thing in the world."

I shared this book with children for the first time in a class of 4th graders at a city school that I visited once a week. These children were not book-oriented, and the purpose of my visits was to help turn them on to reading. Toward the end of this particular morning's visit, I told them that for the last selection I was going to read them a book quite different from the ones we had been sharing. "It's kind of a quiet book," I told them, and without further comment I began to read. There was silence during the reading, and quiet afterwards as well, which was unusual, because these kids normally had no hesitation in letting me know, one way or another, to what degree they enjoyed a particular selection. I left the room feeling that perhaps I had overreached myself, and that this selection was too far removed from the everyday experience of city children.

Upon my return the following week, I was asked to come to the classroom at 9:45, which was earlier than my scheduled time; the children had a surprise for me. When I arrived at the room, they told me to start reading to them and they would let me know when it was time for the surprise. At precisely 9:59 one of the boys jumped up and shouted: "Dr. Higgins, stop reading and listen. Listen!" We all sat in silence, and then at 10 o'clock the bells of the neighborhood Greek Orthodox church began to ring. When it became quiet again, the same boy acted as spokesman for the class: "Do you know what, Dr. Higgins? We've been coming to this school for four years, and every day those bells rang and we never really heard them—neither did our teacher, neither did our principal. Since you read us that book last week, we've all been listening." Then they began to share with me notebooks filled with all kinds of special sounds: morning sounds, street sounds, night sounds, lunchroom sounds. And they were just beginning to discover "secret, silent" sounds, like snow falling, a cat's dream, a mother's presence in the night, and others. In her book, Byrd Baylor uses only the symbols of her desert environment, but they had relevance for these young city dwellers and helped them discover the world around them, as well as the poetic dimension of everyday experience and their own poetic potential.

Another book by Baylor, *Everybody Needs a Rock*, is also useful for extending children into poetic play. I have a different kind of anecdote to tell concerning it. In this book, another Indian boy gives ten rules for finding a rock, not just any rock but "a special rock that you find yourself and keep as long as you can—maybe forever." Rule number 4 is typical: "Don't get a rock that is too big. You'll always be sorry. It won't fit your hand right and it won't fit into your pocket. A rock as big as an apple is too big. A rock as big as a horse is MUCH too big." After I mentioned the book in a graduate class, a young librarian said, "Oh, Dr. Higgins, that's a stupid book. My library is discarding it." Always looking for a bargain, I asked her if I could have the discarded copy. The following week she brought it to class and I saw immediately why it seemed to her a "stupid" book. The Dewey Decimal number on it was 552—the classification for geology!

My first response was one of sadness, for here was another piece of evidence demonstrating how far removed some adults are from an appreciation of the storyteller's and poet's contribution to the educational process. At the same time, however, I must admit I was both amused and delighted to see once again that the playful approach of the writer of children's literature had defied a classification scheme.

THE WRITERS I HAVE been discussing would never think of themselves as environmental educators, but they do contribute to nature education in the deepest and broadest sense. Their books are not written for bookworms who stay forever closeted indoors. This is the literature that calls you out— as Rachel Carson says in *The Sense of Wonder*—to "the lasting pleasure of contact with the natural world ... available to anyone who will place himself under the influence of earth, sea and sky and their amazing life." These are writers who understand the way young children experience nature, and the role these experiences can play. Loren Eiseley put it this way:

> I remember now the yellow buttercups of the only picnic I was ever taken on in kindergarten. There are other truths than those contained in laboratory burners, on blackboards, or in test tubes. With the careful suppression of age, the buttercups grew clearer in my memory year by year. I know that I have been in some degree created by those lost objects in the grass. (Eiseley, *The Mind as Nature*)

Richard Lewis

A WILDERNESS OF THOUGHT
Childhood and the poetic imagination

> The blur of light
> conquers the dark.
> I awake dazzled.
> — David, age 11

THE WIND WAS SCURRYING across the streets of New York, and the children had just arrived at school. I'd recently begun to work with children in poetry and drama, and that morning I had the good fortune to begin my day in a large open space of a room with a group of 10-year-olds. We gathered ourselves in a small circle and spoke of the rush and impatience of the autumn air that seemed to have brought us there. I asked everyone to take their arms and imitate the wind's movement, and it was instantly clear that we needed more elbow room—so I suggested we get up and move like the wind. What I thought might turn into bedlam was suddenly a wonderfully expressive dance in which each child's arms and legs, hands and feet were turning and moving in individual ways, as if they had found something in the wind that they already knew.

When it seemed appropriate to slow down, I asked everyone to find a space on the floor and, if the image of the wind was still clear to them, to write down what they had seen and felt. Afterward, a boy named David came up to show me what he had written:

Richard Lewis

To Be Alive

It was there
Something—happened
What was it
A bird
A fish
A lizard
Was it the girl
Listen.
I hear it again
It is the wind
Wind.
It created me
I am its friend
The wind lives
in a secret garden
far away from me
It comes and I sleep
Sleep and the wind and I
drift to air.

Certain pieces of writing, certain gestures of thought that children share with us can become emblematic—they are entryways to understanding the power of a child's way of gathering insights. In many instances, the child is not even aware of what he has said and will simply shrug if one tries to praise or compliment him. David's writing provided, for me, one of those emblematic moments. What he verified and illustrated was the act of imagining, particularly for children, as a bodily experience— as well as the ways that language, both spoken and written, thought and dreamt, is nurtured and embedded in the imagination. We are creators of images and caretakers of the images we perceive and communicate; it is the *play* of our imagining that allows us to inhabit aspects of the world seemingly distant from ourselves. Certainly David demonstrated this when he wrote without hesitation, "Sleep and the wind and I / drift to air."

This ability of children to easily enter into the life of something other than themselves—to exchange their own mind for the mind of another—grows not only out of their innate playfulness, but out of a fluidity and plasticity of thought that is, in many ways, an inborn poetic gift. It is, perhaps, a way of seeing in which the seer does not distinguish between herself and the *nature* outside of her, an imaginative grasping of the whole of life before it becomes separated into subject matters and academic disciplines. One might think of it as a wilderness of thought that encompasses a multitude of growing worlds, each connected and dependent on the other—a truly ecological means of thinking and perceiving.

Here is 10-year-old Arlanda from New York:

It looks very bad to be an old tree trunk. You are all broke up.
And little animals coming into me making homes.

And 8-year-old Philmore from Liberia:

I saw the road. It was sitting down. It was brown and rocky.

When one looks at what Arlanda and Philmore wrote, it is clear how the mind of the child and an event or object from outside of the child are subtly and gently brought together. This means of expressing and interpreting the world is not something that is taught, but a spontaneous way of explaining that *what is of me is* also *what is happening around me.*

Certainly this is true of Marilyn from New Zealand, who wrote lyrically and suggestively, when she was seven years old, of this shared mind between an insect and herself:

Nothing is better than the song the cricket sings. The sound of the cricket brightens my feelings and makes me sing too. My mind is the cricket's mind and I wish I was a cricket. Hop, hop the black cricket. The cricket pokes out his feelers and I can hold them and the song of the cricket is my mind.

And it is true of Adrian, who, after I had handed a stone to each child in his 5th grade class, wrote:

> The things in my stone want to speak. But they try by the way they build their things, the way they act, the way they react to each other, by their movement, by their joy.

So much of this childhood ease with both the visible and invisible, what we know and don't know—the pure sense of expectation and delight in the mystery of what is happening and about to happen—is not only a function of our mind's ability to balance opposites through the equipoise that is our imagination, but also a way of experiencing the world poetically. I don't mean a poetry of verse and poems, but a poetic understanding that allows us to stand, for instance, in the middle of a stream and say nothing, and yet to feel, if only fleetingly, a sense of how we and the flowing water are of one being. Or to walk down a city street and accidentally walk through the shadow of a tree that seems to move with us, to want to follow us— an expectation, an incandescent moment of which we are suddenly made aware. Each is only an instant, but an instant that carries with it a form of knowledge accessible to children and adults alike, one we rarely include in our current estimates of intelligence or achievement. This awareness should not be seen as a lack of development or a passing innocence, but as a container of thought that we carry with us over a lifetime. Within it, we, the stream, the tree, and the tree's shadow share the same language.

OVER FIFTY YEARS AGO, in an essay titled "The Mind as Nature," the noted anthropologist Loren Eiseley wrote, "If the mind is indigenous and integral to nature itself in its unfolding, and operates in nature's ways and under nature's laws, we must seek to understand this creative aspect of nature in its implications for the human mind." His challenge has certainly been taken up, especially in recent research on the cellular and chemical pathways of our thoughts and actions. What I believe Eiseley was also hinting at was the *nature* of the imagination—in particular the biology of the imagination—not only in terms of its functioning but as a natural process directly related to our own growth and understanding.

Much of children's art and writing shows that there is a process of "unfolding" in their thoughts and feelings that lucidly mirrors the interlocking molecular structures of biology, the mind that is nature. For many children, it is not uncomfortable or unusual to see the wind or a stone as alive, the grass as dancing, or the rain as having a face, like 4-year-old Adrian observed:

> The rain screws up its face
> and falls to bits.
> Then it makes itself again.
> Only the rain can make itself again.

This is not simply a matter of anthropomorphizing or cartooning but of truly experiencing the processes of nature as part of oneself. It is the same innate poetic and mythic instinct that allows a Bushman in South Africa to sing:

> New moon, come out, give water for us,
> New moon, thunder down water for us,
> New moon, shake down water for us.

Or an Inuit woman in the Arctic to sing:

> Day arises
> From its sleep
> Day wakes up
> With the dawning light
> Also you must arise
> Also you must awake
> Together with the day which comes.

Or this 7-year-old child, writing on the back of his drawing of the sun:

> The sun
> warms
> me so
> much.

Each joins the human with the outer world—the natural phenomena of ourselves with the phenomena of nature outside of us—and creates an interchange, a melding of one nature into another.

HOW OFTEN DO WE REMEMBER, or still hear, one child asking another child: "Can you be the mountain, and I'll be the bird?" Or a child playing by herself in the corner of a room, becoming all the parts of her inward story—a cat, the thunder, a sudden rainbow, maybe even someone calling from an open door. While one could argue that this kind of play is fast disappearing because of the distractions of television and digital devices, most children still have a yearning for it—to enter this theater of possibilities and the intimacy of its dreaming and wondering.

How many times have I gone into classrooms that are equipped with the best and latest of technologies and quietly taken from my small, wooden box a robin's feather, a broken twig, a spiraled seashell, a leaf just fallen from a tree, and held each of them up, each a singular species of being, asking how might we feel if we were that twig, that leaf, that feather or shell? And how many times have I been showered with responses that are always urgent and playful, seeking to find the life of a seemingly inert object through the child's own inward imagining? In some improvised gathering of thoughts, the children and I have found together this other kind of poetry, a conversation of sorts that shapes its own way of meaning—different, perhaps, from the everyday instructions of learning, but equally pertinent to the nature of who and what we are and the nature in which we exist.

One such experience took place with a 6th grade class in Queens, New York. Over a period of ten weekly sessions, I asked the children to enter a memory of an actual meadow, one I myself had walked through the previous summer. Part of my challenge was to see how, particularly as children of the inner city, they might be able to imagine the meadow I had experienced and incorporate it into their own imagined meadows. As I told them the story of walking through the mountains of Colorado and finding myself in a large, green meadow surrounded by hills, I also spoke of how, through those meadow-like spaces of our own imagining, we are able to see not only with our outward eyes, but with our amazing inner sight as well.

A pivotal moment in our conversation came when I began to speak of the ominous storm clouds I saw coming toward me as I walked in the meadow. Perhaps it was the mention of the storm, or the way my voice reflected this change of weather, but it was suddenly apparent from the children's eyes and the way they were following the curves and gestures of my telling that they too were also seeing, also remembering, also becoming a part of the landscape and weather I was encountering. I spoke of my fear, my feeling of getting lost—and at a certain point, I asked them what they thought I was afraid of. They quickly responded, as if they were in the meadow, months earlier, with me:

"You were lost in the mountain . . ."

"It was getting dark and you were so scared of like your imagination about the bear or something and everything. Yup, you were scared of that. About your imagination."

"Thunder and lightning . . ."

I realized then, as they spoke up, that we had crossed a boundary. They were no longer bound to an empirical, textbook way of thinking but had begun to trust what, in effect, was the fertile language of their inward seeing—their ability to find this playful part of themselves that could enter into the nature of both their own imaginations and mine. And from there we could begin to explore the innate poetry of this nature—its earth and sky, its growing and changing, its beginnings and endings, its ability to gather and sustain the thoughts that linger and sustain us.

Over the remaining sessions, using writing, drama, and art as our means of expression, the children began to inhabit their own meadows. I gave each child a small, dried flower to hold, touch, and smell. And it wasn't long before wind and air, moons and suns, light and darkness, grass and trees, insects and birds—yes, even clouds and storms—became the living poetry that was their meadow, this nature that was themselves and that they so generously acknowledged and shared with each other.

> My meadow is beautiful.
> It has doves,
> Morning Dew
> And my laughter.
> > – Aisha

> My meadow feels like
> The gala of all meadows.
> There are roses blooming,
> Buttercups growing,
> Daisies smiling,
> Pansies swaying in the wind,
> Black-eyed susans growing...
> > – Dwayne

> Mmm ... I smell that smell. I feel like
> a reindeer ready to rest in a free world,
> waiting for my mother to feed me so I can
> rest.
> > – Baholoame

The slither of light is very beautiful.
As I look through it I can see the world.
        – Jennifer

I am the grass.
I am the still.
I am the sleepy.
I am the quiet.
Oh, yes, I am the grass...
and the still ...
and the sleepy ...
and the quiet ...
Oh, yes, I am the grass
And with this I say goodnight.
        – George

CONTRIBUTORS

Stephanie Hanes is an award-winning journalist who has traveled extensively to Africa, the Caribbean and many locations in the United States. She contributes to numerous periodicals including regular cover stories for the *Christian Science Monitor,* and she launched the popular Modern Parenthood blog on the CSM website. Stephanie teaches the Sharp Journalism seminar at the College of William and Mary, and she is currently working on a non-fiction book about conservation and culture clash in Southern Africa. Stephanie Hanes resides in Andover, MA, with her family.

James E. Higgins was Professor and Chairman of the Department of Early Childhood and Elementary Education at Queens College of the City University of New York. Prior to that he worked as a public school librarian and spent many happy hours reading aloud to generations of New York City school children. Jim's book, *Beyond Words: Mystical Fancy in Children's Literature,* drawn from his doctoral thesis at Teachers College, Columbia, treats the work of C.S. Lewis, J.R.R. Tolkien, W.H. Hudson, George MacDonald, and Antoine Saint-Exupéry. Jim Higgins died in 2009.

Carolyn Jabs is a freelance writer whose work has appeared in numerous magazines and newspapers on topics ranging from family life, ethics and environmental issues to electronic media and the internet. She has long experience in the translation of contemporary issues into language accessible to a broad reading audience. Her monthly column, *Growing Up Online,* appears in many publications on parenting.

Medicine Grizzlybear Lake, also known as Bobby Lake-Thom, is a traditional native healer living in central California. As a Professor of Native American affairs, he taught at Humboldt State University, Gonzaga University and Eastern Montana College. His books include *Spirits of the Earth, Native Healer* and *Call of the Great Spirit,* and he has consulted regularly on matters such as Indian reservation programs, tribal issues, and Indian health, education and social problems.

Richard Lewis is the founder and long-standing Director of the Touchstone Center for Children in New York City. The Center, a non-profit educational institution, celebrates its 45th anniversary this year, and is dedicated to the notion that each person has natural imaginative and creative capacities, and that these can be fostered and encouraged in children through the arts. Programs of the Center explore the role of imagination and poetic thought with special reference to the natural world. Richard's books include *Living by Wonder: The Imaginative Life of Childhood.* He has taught at many colleges and universities, and his work is widely known and admired.

Richard Louv is the well-known author of *Last Child in the Woods: Saving Our Children from Nature-Deficit Disorder* and a subsequent volume, *The Nature Principle.* His writings have served to launch an international movement to connect children with the natural world. Richard helped to found the Children and Nature Network and he is now Chairman Emeritus. He has lectured widely in this country and elsewhere. The notion to "leave no child inside" has struck a respondent chord with numerous grassroots organizations here and abroad, and it serves as a genuine source of inspiration, motivation and hope for many.

Kelly McMasters is a writer and teacher. *Welcome to Shirley: A Memoir from an Atomic Town,* an account of the impact of Brookhaven National Laboratories on the surrounding communities, was the basis of a documentary film, *The Atomic States of America,* a Sundance selection in

2012. Kelly's essays, reviews and articles have appeared in many periodicals. She currently teaches at Columbia University in the undergraduate writing program and the School of Journalism. Her spare time is spent gardening with her husband and two small children in northeastern Pennsylvania.

Lowell Monke taught Computer Sciences in the public school system of Iowa for twenty years before earning a doctorate at Iowa State and joining the Department of Education at Wittenberg University in Springfield, OH. Lowell has written extensively on the impact of media on children and is co-author of *Breaking Down the Digital Walls: Learning to Teach in a Post-Modern World.* He was a founding member of Alliance for Childhood and served on its board for ten years. Lowell now resides on Bear Mountain in Colorado where he is finding inspiration for a new book on a very different form for the educational process.

Pattiann Rogers, a highly acclaimed American poet and teacher, has received many awards for her work. She has published fourteen books, most recently *Holy Heather Rhapsody and the Grand Array: Writings on Nature, Science, and Spirit.* Her poetry has won five Pushcart Prizes, two appearances in *Best American Poetry* and five appearances in *Best Spiritual Writing.* Pattiann has taught kindergarten children and held positions at several colleges and universities. The mother of two grown sons, she resides in Colorado with her husband.

George K. Russell is a long-standing member of the Biology Department of Adelphi University in Garden City, NY. He has worked for several decades to urge teachers to avoid invasive use of animals in the teaching of Biology. His college-level manual, *Laboratory Investigations in Human Physiology* (MacMillan), directs a study of the student's own physiology without a need to kill frogs, turtles and small rodents. George was one of the founders of *Orion* magazine and served as its Editor-in-Chief from 1982–2002. A chief interest is the natural history of his own backyard on Long Island.

Scott Russell Sanders is Professor of English Emeritus at the University of Indiana. His many books and essays are widely known and greatly esteemed. *A Conservationist Manifesto,* published on Earth Day 2009, addresses what Scott holds to be the greatest challenge of our time, how to shift from a culture based on consumption to one based on caretaking. A volume of his essays, *Earth Works,* was published in 2013 and has received high praise. Scott continues to lecture and work with young writers.

David Sobel is a leading figure in the efforts to establish "place-based education" in the mainstream of American pedagogics. His books include *Beyond Ecophobia: Connecting Classrooms and Communities; Children's Special Places, Exploring the Role of Forts, Dens, and Bushes in Middle Childhood,* and *Wild Play: Parenting Adventures in the Great Outdoors.* As a senior faculty member in the Department of Education at Antioch University New England in Keene, NH, David lectures and consults widely on children and their connection to the natural world.

SUGGESTIONS

THE FOLLOWING LIST of suggestions is provided for readers wishing to work in the spirit of the essays presented here. Other ideas, too numerous to mention, can be found through an internet search.

1. The updated and expanded edition of Richard Louv's *Last Child in the Woods: Saving Our Children from Nature-Deficit Disorder* (Algonquin Books of Chapel Hill, 2008) provides a detailed list of "101 actions we can take." We endorse with equal enthusiasm the Children and Nature Network (www.childrenandnature.org) co-founded by Louv. The masthead of this organization proclaims: "Together we can create a world where every child can play, learn and grow in nature in their everyday lives."

2. David Sobel has written *Beyond Ecophobia: Reclaiming the Heart in Nature Education* and several other books relating to direct nature experience, and these provide a solid foundation for what has come to be known as place-based education. Other authors of note include Joseph Cornell, Joseph Bruchac, Lenore Skenazy, and Susan Linn.

3. The Alliance for Childhood (www.allianceforchildren.org) provides helpful guidance for parents and teachers and is committed to the notion that "active play is so central to child development that it should be included in the very definition of childhood." Two of their publications, *Fool's Gold: A Critical Look at Computers in Childhood* and *Adventure: The Value of Risk in Children's Play* are essential reading for all those concerned with the future of childhood. Many suggestions from the Alliance

derive from the principles of Waldorf (Steiner) education, and helpful ideas and materials can be located at the following websites: steinerbooks. org; waldorflibrary.org; whywaldorfworks.org; waldorfbooks.com; and waldorfpublications. org.

4. Jane Goodall, world famous primatologist and conservationist, has built a world-wide organization, Roots and Shoots, as a major undertaking of the Jane Goodall Institute (www.janegoodall.org). With branches in over 130 countries, there are now tens of thousands of children and young adults planting, nurturing, restoring and caring for the natural environment. Local groups exist in many parts of this country and new ones are being formed with regularity. Inspiration for this work can be found in Jane Goodall's autobiographical book, *Reason for Hope: A Spiritual Journey*, and it is a rare young person who will not be profoundly moved by the one-hour documentary, *Reason for Hope: Jane Goodall*, drawn from the book. This video in dvd format is available from the Jane Goodall Institute and online sources.

CREDITS

"Cradle" by Pattiann Rogers and "An Indian Father's Plea" by Medicine Grizzly Bear Lake appeared in *Orion* in Autumn 1995.

Richard Louv's "Leave No Child Inside" was published in the March/April 2007 issue.

David Sobel's "Look Don't Touch" appeared in July/August 2012, and Richard Lewis's "A Wilderness of Thought" is found in the July/August 2013 number.

All essays are © copyright protected.

ABOUT THE MYRIN INSTITUTE

THE MYRIN INSTITUTE was established in 1953 and is dedicated to the notion that we live in a world that holds meaning and purpose for each human being. Fundamental to this view is the idea that a principal challenge of our time is the reconciliation of findings in the natural sciences with a spiritual worldview.

The aims of the Institute, as originally articulated by its founders, are directed toward a genuine renascence of our culture. Specific initiatives have included: understanding and protecting the natural environment, leading to the establishment of the Orion Society and publication of *Orion* magazine; a strong commitment to animal welfare; concern about substance abuse among young people, resulting in numerous publications and the establishment of The American Council for Drug Education; a commitment to education in the broadest sense; a concern for the plight of Native Americans and an appreciation of their traditional wisdom; as well as lectures, seminars and publications on other topics of national importance.

Various publications of the Institute, particularly *Man: The Bridge between Two Worlds* by the Institute's principal founder, Franz E. Winkler, M.D., endeavor to show how each individual can work toward a view in which science, the arts, and spirituality find common ground and mutual enhancement.

The Myrin Institute as a private operating foundation is a 501(c)(3) organization, and donations to assist in its work are fully tax-deductible.

Selected Books from Myrin

A.C. Harwood, *The Recovery of Man in Childhood* (2001) paper $14.95. A survey of child development and the educational system that seeks to develop in children the capacities for imaginative thinking, deepened feelings for other human beings and nature, and the ability to work creatively in the world - the classic work on Waldorf education by a lifelong teacher and lecturer. This book includes an introduction by Professor Douglas Sloan.

Franz E. Winkler, M.D., *Man: The Bridge between Two Worlds* (1960) paper $14.95. A work of remarkable insight and depth as to how education, psychology, human interactions, and international relations can be deepened, and how new understandings can contribute to a profound healing in our time. The notion of trained intuition as a valid mode of cognition is examined and offered as a path of self-development so that individuals can better address the challenges of an increasingly complex and troubled world.

Other Myrin publications are cited on the Institute's website (www.myrin. org), and instructions are provided for their purchase.